GRAMAM GACHAMI

(BACK TO THE BUCOLIC)

A Clarion Call to Return to
Our Traditional Wisdom

K Girish Chandran

Translated by CM Rajan

INSIGHT PUBLICA®

Dedication

Dedicated to the memory of
our beloved parents
Shri Ancheri Raghavan Nair and
Kolarakkandi Sundari Amma.

K Girish Chandran

Born in Poyilkkaaavu village of Koyilandi Taluk in Kozhikode district, K. Girish Chandran had his school education in Poyilkkaaavu High School. After finishing his pre-university course from Government Arts & Science College, he graduated in Chemistry from Samoothiri Guruvayoorappan College, Kozhikode. He did his post-graduation in Political Science at Kozhikode University and had his B. Ed. from the University of Bangalore. He is also a post-graduate in Bioinformatics from the University of Manipal, Sikkim. Besides, he is an M.B. A. with Human Resource Management as his main option. The Cosmopolitan University of U.S. A. has conferred on him a PhD in Education Management.

After serving as a teacher for a few years, since 2008, he has become a resident in Bahrain where he a runs his own educational establishments. He has been an active participant in Educational Seminars and other Conferences in India as well as in other countries. He has visited Countries like the U.K., the U.S. A., China, Russia, Africa, Egypt, Malaysia, Thailand and the Gulf.

His first book, "Swadesh.edu" was published in 2018

His family in Bahrain includes his wife Mrs. Geethakumari, his daughter Nadana, his son-in-law Anand and his granddaughter Janaki.

Content

PREFACE

GIRISH CHANDRAN.

This is an attempt to appraise whether the contributions to Nature and humanity provided by today's internationally widespread system of modern education, Western education, and the social systems it produced have succeeded in making life joyful and whether the systems in the world given by modern science and the like are better than the ancient systems of education that existed in countries including India.

I had prepared a book called 'swadeshi.edu' and published it through 'Insight Publica' in 2018. The book was based on the topic, 'Globalization of Indian Education, Not Westernization of Indian Education'. It was published in English. The book had dealt with topics like 'ancient Indian Education system, the beginning of Education in England', 'the beginning of English Education in India', a comparison between the existing Indian Education and ancient Indian Education' and 'designing a system of Indian Education suitable for the modern age'. This book is written as a sequel to it. It is being written in the 'Corona Age', before which modern science stands in consternation. This age convinces us of the urgent need for rethinking in all the areas including that of Education.

We need to evaluate the replacement of our ancient system of education by the western system of education and its aims and objectives. We also need to examine what in fact provided a happy life for human beings --- whether it was ancient India's achievements or the achievements of the modern age. What has the modern system of education taught us --- self-awareness or arrogance? An honest evaluation shows that it is full-blown arrogance.

The arrogance called 'modern science' has been defying Nature for decades. Along with unethical deeds, we have been engaging ourselves in the arrogant act of declaring ourselves to be the only means of remedy and prevention and also waging war against all creatures of Nature that we dislike.

Though Nature has given us small-scale and big-scale punishments, our arrogance has not diminished a bit. In fact, it is increasing every day. We believe that every resource in Nature is ours only; we, the modern humanity, have the arrogance that every traditional thing in Nature can be transformed into modern. I am sharing here the apprehensions and questions inspired by Nature's horrible punishment for this arrogance I have been experiencing. I have given answers to some of the questions and the rest I have left unanswered. Also, I have discovered a few things which raised many concerns to be addressed. My attempt here is to compare the 'Indian-made' foreign system of education (Western System) with 'Indian-made' Indian system of education (Oriental/Indian system) and to evaluate their merits and demerits in various contexts and areas. So there are many repetitions in various situations. I have written this without any special narrative technique. I present these scattered thoughts for those who want to be free of what they already know.

All of us have been imprisoned by the horror of a small virus called 'corona'. How easily has the invisible little giant 'corona' imprisoned the horrible species of 'modern man' who arrogantly believed that everything including the outer planets is in his control! This species of microbe conquered all including planes, war-equipment, bombs, vehicles and pesticides. Other creatures in Nature like beasts and birds and every living thing we have imprisoned are living free. We experience no freedom in our freedom.

Can't we live at least now decently like these animals... ?

BACK TO THE BUCOLIC', A REVIEW:

SHRIMAD CHIDANANDAPURI SWAMIKAL

It has been a few months since I was asked to write an appreciation for Girish Chandranji's new book, 'Back to the Bucolic' (*Graamam Gacchaami*). As I was busy with reading and writing and as I am usually indolent, I was delayed in reading it. Though I picked it up several times, I got engaged in other matters of urgency. When I found it was time I read it, I took it in my hand. The big question at the end of the preface really touched my heart. That sentence, and through that this book, exerted an undeniable attractive force on me. It led me to read the book attentively. This is the question: "Can't we at least now live decently like these animals?"

The essays in this book are divided into four main headings with many sub-headings. The four main headings are, 'God goes desperate', 'What is education', 'Fear, war and education' and 'What Covid-19 teaches us'. The underlying thought behind all these is that of *Dharma*. The author has meaningfully succeeded in his effort to logically present the argument that Indian education system based on *Dharma* was holistic and oriented towards human development and that today's systems that spread competition, apprehensions and distorted visions are taking us away from *Dharma*. He has presented heart-touchingly the glory and purity of rural mind and rural order of life and the ailments of the city we call 'smart'.

The author, who presents the Indian view that true knowledge consists in the juxtaposition of the knowledge of both the seen (the visible universe) and the seer, lucidly delineates the irony of the modern system of education which focuses only on the seen by brushing aside the seer. He has described in detail how the British had distorted the Indian system of education that helped in total human development by radically changing it and how the new education system, which is anti-human development, has been destroying individualities and generating market products of robotic humans who act in accordance with someone else's orders and decisions. The book reveals before us how, through the media of curriculum and 'dead questions', the modern system of education destroys individualities which should have developed and spread by taking root in one's identity, as trees, which should grow deep and wide, are stunted and kept as objects of exhibition in houses. In today's system, only those who are certified by others are considered to have eligibility. We should think about the irony of this system in which an insightful traditional doctor cannot be a doctor or a great singer cannot be a teacher of music. We can really experience the image of the breaking down of bridges and buildings, constructed by those who gained excellence by means of certificate, before the sky-high towers pulsating with life that were subtle in its imagination and created by a system that had acknowledged an education nurturing innate talents and that had handed over the wealth of traditional experience from generation to generation. Realizing the drawbacks of the system that has created a social mind obsessed with consumerism, we have to beat a retreat towards our identity, towards a holistic vision in which there is no division between the physical and the metaphysical. We should be able to invoke once again the rural mind with its holistic view of human development. We should be able to impart to society that all occupations have dignity and that it is our perspective that lends dignity to labor. There has to be a transformation which eliminates the student who just gives predetermined answers to questions pre-prepared by someone. We have to not only realize but also rectify the evil consequences when the mechanization meant to ease man's life turned into the disaster of the mechanization of society. Thus, we must be able to usher in a complementary harmony between the individual and society, and individual goals and means. The greatness of Mr. Girish Chandran's book is that he has coordinated and presented into a totality his thoughts for making India really India and for the acquisition of the ability for India to execute its mission in the world. In each of his word and sentence, we feel a heart-moving touch ... that which moves the human heart, which is exactly what we miss in the illusory world of consumerism. His exhortation to rebuild the village and to bring back rurality is heart-moving. As it is based on his own experience, it throbs with life. And, that is why he titled his book, 'Graamam Gacchami' (Back to the Bucolic). We don't want the disaster called 'smart city' anymore; let the purity of 'smart village' spread all over. If the world can accept this great message and recognize the heart in these descriptions, I would say we are 'blessed'.

His thoughts save us from the bad state in which the numbers and external trappings of hospitals are considered the standard of health; they save us from the present social and individual situation of fear, war and competition; they also save us from the social diseases caused by the 'disposable' culture and lead us into the Arsha Mantras which, in turn, make us rich and victorious in every sense. These virtuous thoughts must definitely be presented before our society that has lost its thinking prowess. This is a noble attempt. This book will definitely enlighten our society. I wish him all the best.

EDUCATION AND HUMAN LIBERATION

M. A. BABY

Education comprehensively impacts human lives and the world they live in. If this is so, what is the role of economic and social infrastructure, relations of production and ownership of the means of production in life and society? Of course, they play most vital roles. But excellent education and its widespread reach are imperatives for the growth and sustenance of an equitable social system. The ruling powers have always manipulated education to sustain an unjust society for their exclusive appropriation. Lord Macaulay's project of imparting English education to a select class of Indians is a despicable example of administering the empire with the contrived support of a handful of natives schooled in the language and traditions of the Empire. But the impact of such education on Indian history was more pervasive than what was construed by Macaulay. Ironically enough, the project which was intended to keep the majority of Indians under subjugation turned out to be an instrument of their liberation as well. New thoughts and ideas about an equitable society through inclusive development would directly and indirectly get transmitted through the new education, through the process of dialectics, which would also ultimately contribute towards undoing the colonial project. This is similar to the impact made by capitalust class , who take upon themselves the responsibility of inadvertantly organizing workers by deploying them in huge factories and other large scale production sites, thereby providing the opportunity and idea to workers to organize themselves.

Since education plays a major role in life and society it is important for each generation to clearly conceive the methods of acquisition and use of education. There should be proper understanding about changes to be made by each generation in the educational system for its growth and sustenance. There are diverse views among educationalists regarding the direction of changes. The three predominant streams of thought in this field may be roughly stated as follows.

1. 'Education as a tool', which favors the perpetuation of upper-class values to which Western or Eastern educational philosophies adhere to.
2. 'Resource-training', which holds that the objective of education is to train human resources to make them available for multifarious activities involved in large scale production and service sector.
3. 'Education for liberation', which proposes that education should discover and develop students' innate talents ,interests and values and enable them to find work suitable for themselves and society as a whole in an atmosphere of harmonious give-and-take with Nature.

We have different yardsticks for assessing educational growth. We know that even in the so-called developed countries, there is an increase in starvation-deaths, suicides and crimes, emanating from deep distress of the people. In the same way, we also understand that along with big indices of educational growth, there is a parallel growth in illiteracy, unemployment and underemployment. In short, the existing situation is very unjust inequitable and complicated.

This book penned by my friend Dr. Girish Chandran is a discussion on these grave problems. It throws up many significant ideas which I agree with and many other views with which I disagree. However the ideas presented in this work cannot be ignored by anyone with some genuine interest in the future of humankind.

What are the basic objectives of education? Imparting knowledge is one of its fundamental objectives. Imparting skills for work for self realisation and societal needs is also equally important. Developing physical fitness and a healthy lifestyle cannot be ignored either. It is vital that as individuals and as social beings, students should be instilled with positive values of life, a sense of freedom and justice ,scientific temper ,concern for the fellow human beings ,

lifelong commitment to the concept of coexistence of humankind and nature .

If any one of these objectives is ignored, both individual and social life will become chaotic and anarchic.

As we know, since the times of ancient Greek, Roman, Indian, Inca, Chinese, Babylonian, Sumerian and Mesopotamian cultures and civilizations, there has been remarkable germination of ideas about education. Though it would be intriguing to examine which one of those ideas is more ancient, such an investigation is not inevitable. Today, it is scientifically proved that each child has an inherent talent and that a model system of education should have the means to discover and promote it.

Historically, it is only in the modern times that the right of every individual to learn in accordance with his or her aptitudes and social needs has been accepted. Every society (even the pre-modern society) had people branded as slaves and Dalits who are treated as outcastes. The system of caste/economic reservation prevalent in modern societies gives them an opportunity to surpass their inadequacies resulting from the accumulated limitations imposed on them through denial of educational opportunities. Such positive interventions could only partially correct the colossal backwardness inflicted on the depressed and dispossessed classes . Lot more needs to be done scientifically and systematically in this respect to ensure social justice .

There are still different forms of discrimination in the field of education and it is one of the biggest challenges we face today. Yet, the winds of transformation have brought in the message of universal education, loud and clear. It is also important to bring about a total transformation in this field by scientifically evaluating the merits of different concepts of education. The book under review is one which would help us make an informed discussion about vital choices available for us. This book poses the question whether our education has imparted self-awareness or self-conceit. The author also argues that it is relevant to investigate the tragic consequences of unscientific interference with Nature. I totally agree with the author's emphasis on environmental concerns as very fundamental in today's world. World today fervently discusses the fractured success of COP26 related to Global warming and Climate change. This is a matter of life and death, literally and figuratively.

It is quite natural to look up to the *Upanishads* in our search for the roots of Indian education. When we look for the sources of our educational system, we will come across Buddha and Mahaveer. With a historical perspective, the author reminds us that the ancient Indian education and philosophy had given equal weightage to both materialism and spirituality. The ancient Indian approach of acquiring knowledge from diverse sources, i.e., a part of the learning directly from the master, another part from oneself, yet another part from one's life-situations and the last part in course of time is very scientific. The ideas in the Thaitthireeya Upanishad, similar to those in the theory of critical pedagogy, may even surprise us.

But various forms of Brahmanism have appropriated these ideas for their exclusive welfare. Caste-discrimination in our education system has stunted and rusted our progress in the creation of knowledge and its dissemination. I do agree that there are different views in regard to appropriate approaches to education. I totally agree with the author's view that a free, fearless and scientific system of education that nurtures everyone's inherent talents to their maximum should be the ideal that we aspire to materialize.

There is a long list of education-related apprehensions in this book, most of which relate to examinations. The author is concerned about the fears of parents more than the fears of the learners. There is no doubt that learning should be a joyful activity for parents and teachers as well as for students. But the competitive values of the present have taken the joy out of education, which is now reduced to a cut -throat rat-race for success. Acquisition of knowledge should be a fearless pursuit. It is only when your educational endeavor is fearless that you realize how much you have learnt and how much not. Such an approach makes education a sustainable process of gaining self-confidence, joy and creativity. As the philosopher- cum mathematician Bertrand Russell said, "Failure of fear is the beginning of knowledge."

The author observes that the anti-people and anti-nature system of education world over would destroy both, making human life impossible on this planet. The author also cogently argues in favor of traditional medical practices, organic farming and preventive treatment over curative treatment. Most people would agree with this, even though some may still disagree. The writer has pointed out the need for technological interventions for the growth of education. He also puts forth the idea that the services of experts, as visiting professors, should be available to all students. Such an experiment was tried in Kerala during 2006-2011, when inter-university study centers were set up (Kerala is the first Indian State to start such a system of study and research in state universities). I remember the famous maestros in music, who had no university degrees, imparting the wealth of their knowledge in music to the new generation of music students. Inviting the mathematical genius, Padmakumar, who had no formal degree, to do study and research at the Kerala School of Mathematics in Kochi Science and Technology Institute (Now, A. P. J. Abdul Kalam University) was a bold and, at the same time, rare attempt.

The book has certain ideas with which I beg to disagree.

This is self-evident to anyone who knows my views. I will give just one example of my disagreement with the author. On a visit to Maharshi Mahesh University in the U. S., the author had seen many halls for meditation, which was part of the learning program. He opines that meditation should be an integral part of education. But I prefer the practices of scientific analysis and internal dialogue as part of learning by reading, seeing, listening and experiencing. Maybe, meditation aids some people in learning, despite my reservations.

Education is a critical factor for the future of Kerala, India and the world. There has to be a huge change from its present structure and content. It has to be an education that is democratic, secular, and knowledge-based; it should have human values and dignity of labor at its core; it should also maintain social and natural harmony and uphold justice and equality. How this can be achieved is something that can be formulated only through a broad, democratic discussion. This book contains several good ideas which will assist such discussions.

Mr. Girish Chandran had incorporated a few of my observations in his earlier book on education. I had thought that he would not seek my collaboration in his further endeavors in education. But he has now given me another opportunity to express myself through this new book. I would place on record my loving gratitude for his abiding friendship and academic collaboration. I hope that the book would be read and discussed widely.

IN SEARCH OF THE SHEEN OF A GOLDEN RAY

Dr. C. SHREEKUMARAN

Leaving home years ago on one's own interest, roaming freely abroad, when you return home in the eventide of your life, there is your village... like your mother who keeps her grief and grievances like embers in her heart without letting anyone know them and waits for hearing your footsteps and for cooling her eyes with your sight. And, her overflowing incomparable love doesn't hurt you even with questions she kept in her heart about your well-being: Where did you go? Why did you go? Where were you all this time? What did you achieve? In this time of your reunion, flowers, tender coconuts, bovine milk and fresh honey and the like arrange a warm treat for you. The sweet generosity of the diverse tastes of fruits, the purity of uncontaminated vegetables and the immaculateness of unadulterated farm produces, each of them showers solace on you like the unexpected summer rain.

The wind that arrives punctually like a dear girlfriend without slipping away from the hill, the endearing twitter of birds, the rhythms of warbling rivers and the romantic expressions of vegetation, all of these embellish the hospitality. The trees that provide man till they die, (though he is bent on killing them, these fellow beings of his) not only with the fundamental needs of food, shelter and cloth but also with the fragrance of unkissed flowers, breeze, shade, the murmur of leaves and naturally made drinks impart to you a heavenly feeling like the Tree of Wish. Yes, this bucolic belle who is as beautiful as the glow of a golden ray is the very granddaughter of Mother Nature who speaks a lot without speaking.

After you have tripped your foot in the darkness of temptation while you were trapped in the colorful frills of the city, after you have chased the illusory golden deer, and after the sounds of the horse hooves of your fervent youth have subsided, you look back only to find some panting, disillusionments and just an ambition to return to your village. When your spirit is preoccupied with that ambition, your flesh finds it difficult to disobey. When the actor retires to the greenroom after the drama of life is over, the tired actor is forced to make up his mind: Let me go back to my village. He tries for the redemption that will take him to the ever-free, ever-pure and enlightened supreme soul. I think man's pure ambition to return to the village can be regarded as similar to the individual soul of the Vedantins.

When Dr. Girish Chandran published in English his earlier book on Indian education, 'swadeshiedu. in ', I had written a note along with my father Dr. C. Krishnan Namboodiri (A Sanskrit Science researcher, he left for heaven last year). Maybe, it was because of that he happened to ask me to write a note on his new book 'Graamam Gacchami' (Back to the Bucolic). The author's effort to present diverse ideas in different languages in a logical and contemporary way is commendable. Let me first share my hope that there will be more books with such new ideas from this author in times to come.

With this note I only intend to plant a few signposts which will help the reader to enter the diversity of the flowers of ideas that the author tries to cultivate in the courtyard of the reader's heart.

The beginning of the book became auspicious as the author has presented Osho's apt sentence that God resided in man as He wanted to conceal Himself from man. While the author was comparing the Eastern and Western Education Systems, he has chronologically presented things such as its beginning in England and Churchill's view of education. He observes that the ancient Indian education system was not only religious and spiritual but also materialistic. In this context, he quotes the Sanskrit verse, "Quarter of it from the master ..." Let us take an example to elucidate this from a mathematical point of view: Suppose you have to eat an apple by leaving half of it every time. First, you eat a half of it; then the half of that half and so on. If you eat in that order, the sequence you get will be, 1/2+1/4+1/8+1/16+1/32 + ...< 1 (If you add like this, the sum will be less than 1). If it goes in this way, you will not be able to eat a whole apple.

Now let us look at the meaning of the Sanskrit verse:

> 'From the master, a quarter
> From the student himself, a quarter
> From the situation in life, a quarter
> And in course of time, a quarter'

In the last case, it is only mentioned, 'in course of time. (How much time or is it life-long is not mentioned)

When omniscience is impossible, it is difficult to reach wholeness or 1. Hence, 1/2+ 1/4 + ... < 1 –

The author examines the Western education system in the light of Macaulay's ideas and compares it with the ancient Indian educational philosophy. The traditional Indian lore testifies that masters like the seers (in epics, philosophies and *Upanishads*) used to answer any question from their disciples. In contrast, in the modern educational method, the students ought to answer the questions posed by the teachers. The author points out that if it is in the reverse, the teachers will find it difficult to survive. He unveils the excellence of the ancient seers' educational method. It is also to the credit of Oriental method that the evaluation must come from society and not from examinations. Ramayana offers us the evidence that the ancient seer, Vishwamitra used Sri Rama's learning to protect his Yaga from demoniacal powers.

The observation that teachers say what they want to say and not what students want to hear is remarkable. Researchers and seekers of knowledge can study the well-thought-out ideas of Steve Jobs, Thomas Edison, Henry Ford and Bill Gates. The definitions correlating these ideas may make the readers think that remembrance and forgetfulness are birds of the same feather. In his musing on modern education, the author does not deny that self-conceit may emerge from self-awareness. He records not only the limitations of modern education but also the indigenous nature of Indian Art, Music, Architecture, Yoga and Martial arts along with their glory.

Because 'entrance tests' eliminates a majority, the author likes to rename them 'exit tests'. Readers will definitely find inspiration as the author puts forth his ideas with illustration in

the light of his experiences. The analysis of terms like fear, war, course-study and meditation will help attract the modern world. What is revealed here is the author's breadth of ideas, his depth of reading, his expertise in research and skills of language.

The suspicion whether an abundance of facilities will turn the village into a city is like the anxiety of a mother who fears whether her son will leave her for the city when he grows up and gets married. Since such a situation is not impossible, the suspicion cannot be brushed aside. The village is a center of attraction for both those who were born there and those who were born in city and fed up with it. But we should also see that, in a world of people with diverse tastes, there must be some who don't like the village. But even they will agree that the village is an immortal organic store.

In his English story, 'Home Coming", the world famous poet and Nobel laureate Rabindranath Tagore heart-touchingly presents the teenager Pathik Chakravarthi who yearns for returning to his village to celebrate with his old playmates. As for Kerala, the poets' words have reflected the rural glory and the nostalgia for the village. Kuttipurath Keshavan Nair, in his 'Village Virgin' sings, 'The city full of affectations is poor and the village full of good is rich'. And the recently deceased O. N. V. Kurup, after singing about the sweetness of well-water, the desire to be the playmate of the peacock-feather-clad child and the song of the cuckoo, found relief in singing, 'Though I know these desires are futile, I still just desire them.' He comforted not only himself but also the entire Malayalees. The song Anil Panachooran wrote for the movie, 'Arabikkatha' still echoes in young singers' heart. This book gives me the occasion to remember not only the idyllic songs but also all the precious sights and sounds of my childhood days. All the indigenous festivals like Vishu, Onam and Thiruvatira and all the childhood colors and plays remain indelibly in my memory.

In the discourse of today's world, are the words like 'rustic', 'natural' and 'brutal' are misunderstood in a way it hurts the rural hearts? It is in this context that Mr. Girish Chandran's noble book, Graamam Gacchami (Back to the Bucolic) becomes remarkable and relevant. For this journey to the village to be meaningful or fruitful a little preparation will be helpful. These lines of Vailoppilli will be helpful:

> "Let there be on our mind the bucolic purity,
> A little fragrance, kindness and country flowers."

GOD GETS DESPERATE

There is a beautiful story that Osho relates to his disciples:

God created humans and all other creatures. Having finished the very long process of creation, He retired to relax. Animals and other creatures were content with the life they had obtained, but humans alone were not content. One after the other they visited God and kept complaining. They did not let Him have any rest. So He went into hiding, but wherever He hid Himself, they sought him out. Eventually, the angels gave counsel to God,

"Lord, even if you hide yourself in any nook and cranny of this universe, humans will seek you out. You have to find such a place as they will never be able to search you out."

The angels, after ruminating for long, presented a suggestion before God.

"You had better reside in humans. They will never look inside themselves."

God also felt that the angels were right. Since that day He started residing inside the humans. And, they started an unending search all over the world for God who dwells in themselves.

In various ways and through various topics, our modern education, which is really the Western education system, teaches us everything about the world. But it has a colossal flaw that it does not teach us to look into our own selves.

Each child is innocent. If that innocence is at the unconscious level, it will be lost. We will not be able to sustain that innocence for long in this crafty world of today. True, we have to employ the utmost craft in the global market. And, it is to that end that schools, colleges and universities have been built.

But 'real education is yet to be born in us'. Real education will inculcate in us conscious innocence and impart to us genuine awareness. Today's education, however, is killing our innocence rather than enabling it. Though it is declared that modern education is meant for us, the results show a different picture. Is it not well known that a tree is recognized by its fruit?

The whole world today is flawed and chaotic. That itself evinces the drawback of our education. The people we see around us are the offshoot of our education, culture and civilization. The crisis that today's world faces can be surmounted only if the innocence by real education is honored and preserved.

OCCIDENTAL/ORIENTAL EDUCATION

We call education 'modern' since the Western education system was introduced. However, we do have a need to probe whether this modern education system is better than the Indian education system.

We do not have adequate material to help us study the ancient Indian education system. Vedas are the only documents we have. And, among the Vedas, the *Rigveda* is the most ancient. Historians think that it was written about three thousand years before Christ. The magnificence of education before that time can be seen in the competence of Vedic writing.

The education system that had earlier existed in India and other East Asian countries merged with the Islamic education system under the later Mogul rule of seven decades. With the advent of the British rule, in India, the British education system gained strength in popularity and the other two education systems considerably declined.

THE BEGINNING OF EDUCATION IN ENGLAND

Until 597 A.D., when St. Augustine arrived in England, schools were alien to England. The Church needed priests for its services and boys for singing in its choir. It was to that end that, as a part of the St. Augustine Church, the first Grammar School was established in Canterbury in 598 A.D.

THE EDUCATION SYSTEM UNDER THE CHURCH (1100 – 1500 A.D.)

By 1100 A.D., Every cathedral and every collegiate church had its school. In most of the European nations, it was the Church that oversaw education. By the beginning of the fourteenth century, nearly five percent of Europeans acquired education of some sort. It was the church that decided the syllabus and the curriculum. Most of the teachers were the priests and bishops from the collegiums. Arts, Languages and Theology were the main topics taught. Science and other subjects did not receive much consideration.

THE BEGINNING OF EDUCATION IN INDIA

India is a nation with one of the ancient-most cultural traditions of the world. The ancient Indian education system is over five thousand years old. Our Vedas, which were written when the world had no religion, were described by the Westerners as religious texts. Through Western education they monopolized the field of education and depicted the study of Vedas as the study of religion; even we propagated it as such. A culture based on the Eternal Law of Nature, Hinduism was, however, interpreted by them as a religion like the 'Hebraic' one.

The inventions and discoveries our seers made after studying and observing life for thousands of years were reduced by them absolutely to religious beliefs. Besides, it was propagated that Indian education was confined just to spirituality. But we have enough evidence to show that Indian education had emphasized both spirituality and materialism.

One could obviously see the scientific approach in all the sources of Indian knowledge, from the *Upanishads* in the Vedas to the pure sciences. Do not harbor the mistaken notion that scientific approach is the contribution by modern science. Scientific approach is an inalienable part of all streams of Indian thought. Our masters and seers described for the good of the world what they had seen by virtue of their own direct experience. Also, they never insisted on accepting what they had said without questioning.

The words of the masters were given only a quarter of importance in the process of education:

> शनैःपन्थाःशनैर्विद्या शनैःपर्वतलंघनम्।
> आचार्यात् पादमादत्ते पादं शिष्यःस्वमेधया ।
> सब्रह्मचारिभ्यःपादं पादं कालक्रमेण च ॥

"Those who want to travel far, or to explore deeply, or to study or to ascend a mountain to conquer it must proceed leisurely.

A student has to imbibe only a quarter of the things from the masters; he has to find out on his own another quarter; yet another quarter has to be acquired from discussions with others and still another quarter has to be had in the course of time."

This was the way we acquired knowledge. Studies like Economics, Archery, Music, Medicine and Engineering were there as the subsidiary Vedas. We had an educational system that gave equal importance to both spirituality and materialism since the time of Vedic studies.

THE AIM OF EDUCATION: OCCIDENTAL AND ORIENTAL

When the British East India Company, established in 1660, gained ascendancy in India, it started to follow the educational policy similar to that of the French and the Portuguese. Yet, there was a difference. The French and the Portuguese had emphasized the Catholic approach, but the directors and officials of the British East India Company, who were opposed to that approach, gave importance to the Protestant approach in education. In 1659, the Company adopted propagation of religion as its mission and duty. According to the Charter of 1698, the company was permitted to employ

Christian missionaries. These missionaries who arrived by trade-ships started propagating the ideas of the Protestant religion. With a view to encouraging the conversion of people into Christianity and educating those converts, schools were established. The importance given to religion in these schools and the method of teaching students in small batches were little different from the way that existed traditionally in India. But the content and goals were vastly different. The Company's educational aim was to propagate Christianity and to train people to be employed in the company. They also wanted to gain materially and mold a society that would function according to the rules of its law.

Gradually, the British East India Company started to emulate in their educational activities the private missionaries' style of functioning. That was how it started opening English schools.

Among the missionary schools, the opening of the schools of charity was an important step. They were aimed at helping the orphaned children of European soldiers and other helpless European children in India.

When religious propaganda gained strength, it invited protest from people of other religions. Some of the pamphlets released by the Christian missionaries added fuel to fire. As a result, in 1808, the Board of Directors of the East India Company asked it to adopt a secular approach.

British East India Company's policies, which discouraged the missionary activities, had to face stiff opposition in Britain. In 1793, Wilber Force brought it up in the British parliament as a topic of debate. Strikes and protests were organized to move the British government to make legislations for the missionary missions to continue. The main spearhead behind this movement was Charles Grand who was a member of the parliament and one of the directors of the Company. In 1797, he published a book on this. To uplift the people of India, he proposed two important things:

1.Educate them in English medium

2.Convert them into Christianity

MACAULAY'S MINUTES (1835)

Even when they were imposing English education deliberately on Indians, the British had the conviction that Indian education was excellent. Macaulay's Minutes, published in February 1835, testifies to it. The Minutes is one of the fundamental documents in the history of Indian education.

Macaulay had convinced the British government that India could be politically conquered only through cultural and educational domination. So, by establishing English education, Indians had to be convinced that the British education was far superior to their own education. "I couldn't see a single beggar in India after traveling far and wide in the country; they are so rich," he had recorded.

According to the Charter of 1813, it was Macaulay's responsibility to define the kind of education to be implemented in India. It was necessary to elucidate usages in the Charter like 'literature' and 'Indian scholar'. Macaulay interpreted 'literature' as English Literature and 'Indian scholar' as the one who has deeply studied the English knowledge system that includes the philosophy of Locke and the poetry of Milton. Besides, he insisted that Science could be acquired only through the language of English.

THE OBJECTIVES OF WESTERN EDUCATION IMPLEMENTED IN INDIA

1. To eliminate a society that thinks independently and realizes its capabilities on its own
2. To bring up through English education a large society that admires the West
3. To put an end to the transparency and social interference of educational activities. The foremost thing they established to achieve this end was the system of 'certificates'
4. To implement Western syllabi and to create Boards of Examinations
5. To teach what these educational Boards decide as syllabus and to implement a system of examinations in which only those who write the answers given by them to the questions they have prepared will be passed

6. To demolish the Indian traditional system of education by conferring certificates on those students who pass these exams and by bringing in a law which makes only these students eligible for employment
7. To reduce the system education to a system of examinations and to turn these exams into a method of just getting a job and of earning money
8. To limit education to the goal of passing by hook or crook these exams for earning more money, instead of promoting one's talents
9. To create a teaching community of graduates to suit this system
10. To propagate the religion and the rites of the West through those teachers and to limit the control of all the domains into the hands of those graduates, thereby getting the order of the world under their thumb
11. To eliminate independent geniuses and to push them out of the social order of the world
12. To abolish traditional systems of knowledge and streams of thoughts
13. To destroy the individuality of a person to turn him into a money-spinning machine without any sense of ethics
14. To create a society of puppets that obey the government

The very objective of Oriental education that was there since the Vedic studies was different. It never approved of a society that aimed only at material gains and the lure of lucre. Not that it rejected material gains altogether; but the educational system of ancient India had aimed at independent thinking and the realization of individual talents which could be utilized for the welfare of the individual and the society.

HOW TO THINK

If the Occidental education teaches you what to think, the Oriental education trains you how to think. If we are to ask a question, there has to be motivation. There is almost nothing that motivates in the Western education system. We acquire knowledge through questioning. A question born of motivation emerges in the mind of the disciple and the master helps him find out its answer --- that was how our system of education functioned. We can see ample evidence in the Vedas and *Upanishads* of such intelligent students who go in search of teachers and masters to get answers to their questions. For instance, in Mundakopanishad, Shounaka the Mahashala asks Angiras the seer:

"Please teach me that, by knowing which everything is known."

Angiras then explains to him elaborately the very 'secret of self'. This Upanishad has many poetic mantras in it. The master-mantra, 'Truth alone triumphs' appears in this Upanishad:

सत्यमेव जयते नानृतं सत्येन पन्था वितितो देवयानः
येनाक्रमंत्यृषयो ह्याप्तकामो यत्र तत्सत्यस्य परमं नधिानम्॥

"Truth alone triumphs; not Untruth.
The truth to which the divine way leads is one.
Through that way the seers, whose desires are all fulfilled,
Reach the place of Brhama, the ultimate destination of Truth."

Can anyone of the teachers, who have acquired graduate and postgraduate degrees through modern education system, can answer in detail the independent questions of his students?

In the method of Western education system, teachers ask questions and the students answer them. If there is an education system wherein the students ask questions and the teachers have to answer, how many of the teachers will be able to continue their profession?

The primary objective of ancient Indian educational system was an individual's holistic development --- the physical, mental and spiritual development. A people's view of life and its education are inextricably related to each other. Ancient Indians had a sublime view of life, which had reflected in the objectives of their education. They viewed life as a ceaseless stream. Also, our ancient system of education was in close contact with its society.

THE ANCIENT SYSTEM OF EDUCATION

The learning of a student had its commencement with *Upanayan*, the rite of initiation and passage. *Upanayan*, for the student, was the beginning of a new life --- the beginning of formal education. The phase of life after it was called *Brahmacharya* --- a life of abstinence and chastity. The disciple who had sought out his master would live with him and his family as one of its members while learning. This system of learning was known as *gurukula* education --- education at the master's homestead. These homesteads were situated in woods, a long way off the chaotic atmosphere of the world. The lifeline of this system was the spiritual relationship between the master and the disciple.

The *gurukula* system of education was not for mere acquisition of knowledge. The student was trained in all matters needed for success in life. In those days, there was no 'classroom system' in which students of all sizes and shapes were taught alike. The student also used to get trained in a vocation in accordance with his natural flair. He would live his entire educational life as a member of the master's home. As a result, the master had every opportunity to carefully nurture the character of his disciple.

Students of ancient India used to study topics of varied interests. They acquired competence in the Vedas, the Epics, the Legends, Grammar, Biology, Mathematics, Logic, Diplomacy, the Art of Brahma, Phonetics, Meter, Magic, the Art of War, Astrology, Snake-charming, Fine Arts, Music, Dance, Instrumental Music, Sculpting and Medicine.

The method of instruction in those days was dialogic: The disciples would pose questions and the master would answer them with explanations. Also, the rulers of the day had no say in the ancient Indian education.

Masters had a very venerable position in the society. It was the society that gave position of prestige to the teachers and masters. The foremost mission of a master was to mold his disciple into excellence. Our systems of thoughts make it clear about the person from whom one should acquire learning:

अचनिोतचि शास्त्रारथं आचारे स्थापयत्यता।
स्वयमप्याचरेदस्तु स आचार्यःइतास्मृतः॥

"The master is one who apprehends things scientifically, imparts his knowledge easily to his disciple and follows in his life what he preaches."

And, the students must be those who are ever alacritous to imbibe, learn and digest things:

काकदृष्टिर्बकध्यानं श्वाननिद्रा तथैव च ।
अल्पाहारो जीर्णवस्त्रं च एतद्विद्यार्थिलक्षणम् ॥

"The crow's eyes, the crane's concentration, the dog's alertness, moderate eating and simple clothing are the features to be seen in a student."

That is to say that a good student, like a crow, must have the ability to observe his surroundings; he, like a crane, must be able to concentrate on the thing he is doing; like a dog, he must be vigilant even in his sleep; he has to eat in moderation to keep himself fit; and, he must be able to project his personality through simple attire.

The basis for analysis must be the clearly scientific features of knowledge. If it is impossible to analyze on the principle of 'evidence of science', maxims – the sayings of sages – must be taken as evidence. That is because, these are the essence of knowledge the seers have acquired through observations and experience of thousands of years.

Today, what we carry out in India is a second-rate Western educational system. Education has now come to mean 'Western educational system'. Even the oriental countries like India where there was once a strong and exact educational system are competing for more and more westernization. It has come to a situation wherein not only education but also medicine, music, dance, literature and even cuisine are westernized. Our customs and rituals have turned Western and into their religious mode. We celebrate our birthday by cutting cakes and blowing candles. It is the custom in Christianity to consider Sunday the 'holy' day. And, by implementing that belief in the western way in the public domain, we have also made Sunday 'holiday'.

Branding the Eternal *Dharma*, and all the discoveries and educational methods that existed much before the emergence of any religion obsolete and religious, the westerners made a few changes in their curriculum designed for their religious purpose and presented it as 'secular'. They extirpated the independent educational system in ancient India and transformed it into a mere system of government-controlled examination for getting 'certificates'.

Inspired by the free education in the *Ashan* schools (schools run by individual teachers) in Malabar and elsewhere, Bell Andrews, who was a missionary in Madras in those days, established a school called 'Madras College' in his own country, Scotland and implemented a method of education called 'monitoring system'. In those days, Malabar belonged to the State of Madras. Instead of employing more teachers in the *Ashan* schools, the practice was to train senior students of merit to teach new learners. The students used to learn by writing on sand. In those days, education was prohibitive in Britain. So the number of the educated was very few. And, women's education was just nominal. Instead of signing in 'marriage contracts', people simply used to draw the picture of the cross. Bell Andrews, by virtue of introducing an inexpensive system of education, came to be known as 'the father of mass education'. It was this system of education, among other things, that inspired Maria Montessori to introduce the 'Montessori method', her method of Primary Education. She was in India from 1939 to 1946. In 1939, she conducted a 'training course' in the Theosophical Society of Madras and continued the training in many other places including universities before returning to Amsterdam at the age of seventy six.

The westerners were well-convinced of the merit of the ancient Indian system of education before they eradicated and replaced it with Western education. In fact, the Indian system of education had more merits than the Western system of education:

1. The ancient Indian system of education had broader objectives of which the most important was the holistic development of the individual. As a result, the individuals had a holistic view of life and sense of ethics. The objective was not to obtain a 'certificate' for mere employment, as in the modern system of education.
2. The system of Indian education had a method of education free of the control of the government; it was an independent system necessary for nurturing the natural flair of students.
3. There was the facility to select the best teachers for

one to get trained in the best possible way.

4. Education came to an end only when the master was convinced through constant evaluations over a long period of time that his disciple had acquired knowledge; not when a degree was secured through a mere examination.
5. The masters and teachers were competent enough to clarify the doubts and to respond to the questions of their disciples.
6. Since the disciple used to stay with the family of the master as one of its members, he could empirically learn the practical and ethical aspects of life.
7. It was the society that gave the teachers and masters their position of prestige. It was on the basis of their knowledge and discipline in life that they were respected and given their positions; they did not join the profession of teaching on the strength of merely writing an examination. There was a strict 'social auditing' in those days.
8. The motive behind teaching was never monetary. The goal was to mold students into excellence. The student could pay his master anything in accordance with his economic situation.
9. Our ancient system of education was meant to lead one from egoism to self-awareness. It could be seen on closer examination that our system of education was an exhortation against the anti-scientific attitudes such as pride, egoism and ignorance.
10. The ancient system of education gave its students the freedom to accept things only when he was convinced of them as right:

"Will anyone drink from a well that yields brine water,
Even if it was dug by his own father!"

It means that there is no need to accept and respect even one's own father by drinking brine water; there is no need to respect one's masters by accepting their mistakes. That is the message of this couplet.

All the works and discoveries of ancient India are also evidence of the excellence of the educational system of that period. Works such as the Mahabharata, with its twelve hundred thousand verses and over four thousand characters, and the Ramayana attest to the education of ancient days. Veda Vyasa and *Valmiki* were not people of high caste. Krishnadwaipayana aka Vedavyasa and *Valmiki*, who was a hunter called Ratnakara, bear witness to the intellect nurtured by that system of education. The merit was not just in the field of Literature; the scientific discoveries of ancient India were also of the highest standard. *Ayurveda*, which is the world's oldest and most popular system of medicine, is ancient India's contribution to the world. It was after studying the ancient, traditional medicine for thousands of years that Charaka and Sushrutha formulated their treatises. Hippocrates, the father of modern medicine, had mentioned that a great many times.

In ancient India, there were competent scientists and significant discoveries in the fields such as Mathematics, Engineering, Metallurgy, Astronomy and Geography.

Forms of arts like Music and Dance were there well before the modern system of education. It was because of an independent system of education that the inventions and discoveries were made possible in the fields such as Arts, Music, Literature and Mathematics. The modern system of education denies us independent thinking and learning. It is the government that decides how to study, what to study and how long to study. If you pass one or two examinations, wherein you give the answer they want for the dead questions the Boards have prepared, you are given a certificate of qualification. No intelligent student has the right to get out of the frame of the Board of Exams. Any smart student can do only one thing: Get a certificate of excellence from the Board of Exams by rote-learning the answer they give for the dead questions they have prepared. The questions arising from the motivated mind are the live ones; the questions from a Question Bank are the dead ones.

During the days of Freedom Struggle, there were many discussions on national education and there were strong opinions against the Western system of education. However, after independence, the independent system of education was even more damaged. The bureaucracy implemented certain standards that kept society and genius scholars away from the schools. Needless and irrational disciplines were introduced even in private schools and more power was centralized through the bureaucracy. In our social system, the introduction of more disciplinary measures often enables the net of corruption to gain a wider reach.

What role do the intelligence and innovation of a student or a teacher have in a system of education under the government's control which decides everything from what the students should study, what questions the teachers to ask, what answers students should give, which topic students should study at a certain hour to how students should dress? Even the employment of teachers is a joke. Only those who have passed an order of examination under the system of government have the eligibility to teach. If Veda Vyasa, the man who gave the world such wonderful works as the Mahabharata, were alive today, he who wrote the twelve thousand hundred verses would not be found eligible to teach his own Mahabharata in any university of Sanskrit as he lacks the certificate of eligibility from the government. But those teachers who have this certificate cannot write even some twenty verses like him. Thakzhi Sivasankarapillai has no right to teach his works such as '*Chemmenen*' or '*Kayaru*'. My own country cousin, Master Padmashree Chemancheri Kunhiraman Nair is a man who performed *Kathakali* even in his hundredth year. He is not eligible to teach *Kathakali* in any of the government establishment.

Among the educational establishments in our country, Engineering Colleges are the most in number. In the days of yore there were geniuses among the architects and engineers who had built incredible edifices --- geniuses who had built the Ajanta and Ellora caves and the *Taj Mahal*. They had studied architecture and engineering in the traditional way. There are still some people belonging to those generations. They have no eligibility to teach in any institute of architecture or to approve a plan of building to be submitted in a Municipality, the reason being the lack of a certificate of qualification.

Because our modern system of education declines categorically the skill and knowledge of the competent people in every field who have traditionally acquired them, the gains we have made in various fields through centuries are left unutilized.

The obverse of this fact can be seen in the majority of the graduates from the universities who cannot work or show efficiency in their own field of study. A teacher who has a post-graduation and a doctorate in Sanskrit and Literature has never studied any major text in Sanskrit. He cannot write even a few verses. Besides, it is in English that this person has written his research paper on Sanskrit, because the university accepts only the research papers written in English. This is situation of our university degrees. And, the government spends billions for this farce.

There were expert doctors in the medical field in the ancient days. They were people who studied medicine traditionally. The diagnosis, treatment and preparation of medicine were almost always done at the doctor's house. There were many such eminent traditional health-homes in many parts of India. As the modern medicine lobby gained ascendancy, our centuries-old traditional medical knowledge was destroyed through the government's influence. Experts like Padmabhooshan Dr. B. M. Hegde have been harping on the loot and atrocity of the modern medicine of Allopathy. But the government seems to be helpless. Other pharmacies have come under the control of the lobby of English medicine as well.

A friend of mine runs a center for physiotherapy. A number of people with sprains, bruises and fractures come here daily to seek treatment and get cured. The decades-old clinic is run by the second or third generation of my friend's family. There are a few BAMS graduates working at this center. I have enquired of my friend, the owner and chief doctor of this establishment, about these doctors. He says that these doctors are efficient in handling 'data entry' and 'filing'. When I have asked him about their competence in treatment, he says that they need to gain experience for some five or six years. As of now, they have negligible experience in that domain, he says. As far as my friend is concerned, he started his practice only after he had mastered medicinal preparation for 15 years. He treated his first patient under his father's supervision. The treatment at his center is entirely based on the herbs he cultivates in his own herbal garden. Even patients from abroad seek treatment here and leave after complete recovery. The trust earned by this decades-old establishment is far superior to any certificate of graduation. Since the reign of the westerners, they wanted to dominate all the fields from education to health. To that end they decided that only those who have passed their examinations and obtained degrees should have the eligibility for working. Later, even in the non-governmental areas the prohibition of the traditionally trained was enforced. Those who enforced the practice knew very well that the graduates in these fields were not so competent. In the course of time, all the official administrative staff came to be consisted of such graduates. Thus, a large coterie of people, who came to believe certificates of graduation to be the measure of efficiency, was created. They succeeded in transforming our society into a blind, irrational society. Even to this day, our society blindly believes whatever the westerners do is always right.

However, across the world including the western society, a majority of people who stamped their unique individuality are those who have turned their back on formal education. Let us examine a few such cases.

1.STEVE JOBS

Steve Jobs, the American business magnate, was born in 1955. He was the Chairman and CEO of the Apple Company. In 1972 he joined Read College and, in the same year, he dropped out of college. However, he used to visit the college to meet his friends in places such as the canteen. Steve used to explain his reason for his break from education: "Whatever the teacher said in the class was what she had to say; that was not what I wanted to hear. Why should I pay the fees for listening to that?"

None of those who passed with flying colors from Read College could succeed in life so brilliantly as the drop-out Steve.

2. BILL GATES

Bill Gates, the Head of Microsoft, is a drop-out from the University of Harvard. He was a student of Law at the University. But he didn't finish his education. Instead, he followed his own inclination and launched a start-up in the field of IT. The company became one of the supreme companies in the world. If he had graduated as a student of Law from Harvard, he would have remained just a lawyer all his life.

This is one of the drawbacks of formal education: One does not have a chance to choose a subject of one's interest; More often than not, one has to choose a subject one dislikes. "To win big, you have to sometimes take big risks," Bill Gates used to say. Maybe, he could say so because he could break out of the prison of formal education.

3. THOMAS EDISON

A man who keeps silent and wanders with incoherent thoughts --- that was how Thomas Edison's school teachers appraised him. It was such an Edison who founded the 'General Electric', one of the internationally biggest companies. "Many of life's failure are people who did not realize how close they were to success when they gave up," says Thomas Edison.

4. HENRY FORD

Henry Ford, known as the world's automobile billionaire, grew up in poverty and starvation. He never had any formal education. "Thinking is the hardest work to do, that's why so few people are engaged in it," Henry Ford could think so because he was able to fly free in a sky without the fetters of formal education.

All these eminent personalities are people from the West. They became role models by succeeding in life without any formal education but by following their instinct and ability.

What lesson do we learn from their stories? We would reach the acme of success, if and only if we discover and cultivate our capabilities and inclinations. Western Education has a sole objective: acquisition of material gains. The miseries the world today goes through are the tragic consequences of reducing the objective of education to the acquisition of wealth and other material gains. It is high time we reevaluated the aims of and objectives of our education.

WHAT IS EDUCATION?

Ask the people engaged in the field of education, especially teachers, 'What is education?', and the answer you get will be the half-forgotten definitions they learned during their B. Ed days. Ask them what they have learnt from their experience in the field, the answer will be thoroughly disappointing.

I was also fascinated by the various educational ideas when I was doing my B. Ed. The word 'education' has its origin in the Latin word, 'educere' which means to 'draw out' or 'lead forward'. I had found the word and its definitions meaningful.

Mahatma Gandhi had said that the objective of education is to draw out the best in one's body, mind and soul. Is this process being carried out today? Even in this modern age in which modern education rules the roost, many activities questioning its practice have emerged from various parts of the world.

"Education is the discovery of a person's self' --- our formal education is a good example of distorting this idea into erroneous definitions and applications. Our modern system of education has failed not only in discovering one's inner self and enabling one to relate to the world but also in guiding one in accordance with one's needs and nature.

It is not fair to consider someone educated just because for a few years he has passed through the system of training and examination framed by our government. It is equally unfair to consider someone illiterate because he has not had any formal schooling. Today, the world faces the menace of terrorism. A great many of the terrorists are highly educated people from the top universities in the world. Taslima Nasreen, an eminent writer, is of the opinion that poverty and illiteracy are not the breeding grounds for terrorism. According to her, the leaders of terrorism are highly educated ones hailing from well-off families. Today, there is even a catchphrase in vogue - - - 'engineering terrorism'. Things have come to such a state because people believe that education is only a means to gain wealth and material comforts.

It is after spending millions that a doctor often secures his degree. Hence, his only thought will be to recover that amount and collect more money. If he can earn more money by bumping off a patient than by curing many patients, he will definitely kill the patient. An engineer may rather sabotage a building than erect many buildings, if his act of destruction brings him money. Many educational institutions including those in India have turned into centers of anarchy and treason because of the erroneous understanding of educational objective. Today, the system education needs a thorough overhaul globally. Otherwise, a situation will arise in which not only the human society but also nature itself will be damaged.

WHY? WHY? WHY?

Modern science has been able to transform our world dramatically. However, Science has still no answers to fundamental problems. Osho has something to say about how Science and Philosophy deals with this problem. In his book, '*Geethadarshan: Sankhyayoga*', he says: Philosophy always goes in search of an answer to the question, 'why?'. It may arrive at an answer. But, again, the question 'why?' arises in connection with that answer. It may find another answer. But each answer it finds will further raise the question, 'why?'. This questioning goes on *ad infinitum*. Each answer leads to another question. For every answer, we can ask 'why?'. Whatever is the answer, the question, 'why?' persists. Hence, Philosophy is a dead-end.

In contrast, Science never asks, 'why?'. It asks 'what?'. Hence, Science is not a dead-end. Likewise, Religion does not ask 'why?' either. It too asks 'what?'. Therefore, Science and Religion are close to each other. If Science has an enemy, it is Philosophy. Usually, people think that Religion is a kind of Philosophy. But Religion is not a philosophy at all. The meaning of Religion is 'to know'. It asks, 'what?' and not 'why?'. Religion knows that there is an answer to the question, 'What is existence?'It knows that there is no answer to the question, 'Why is existence?'. Science also asks only 'what?'.

If you ask 'What is water?' you will get an answer: Water is made up of hydrogen and oxygen. But if you ask a scientist why hydrogen combines with oxygen, he will ask you to pose that question to a philosopher. He will say that his research in his lab is based on the answer to the question, 'what?'. He will say, "We can show you hydrogen and oxygen combining to form water. If you ask us 'what', we can give you an answer. We can even prove it. If you ask 'how', then also we can give you an answer with proof. But, please don't ask us 'why'. Put that question to either madmen or philosophers.

"However deep we research, we can only know the answer to the question 'what?'. And, later, we will be able to show you the 'how' of it. You know hydrogen and oxygen atoms combine to form water. We know the structure of water. We have also discovered that the atoms are combined." Science is based on the question, 'what?' and the research in the lab is based on the question 'how?'. (*Osho: Geethadarshan; Sankhyayoga*)

How successful has modern Science been in solving fundamental problems? The errors in the implementation of modern science have led the world into miseries. The reason is not just the errors in application. The reason is also its approach mismatching with the laws of Nature.

SOLUTION TO THE PROBLEMS AND COEXISTENCE WITH THE PROBLEMS

Modern Science is a failure both in appraising our problems and in approaching them rightly. Modern Science and Western methods have adopted an impracticable approach to discovering the root causes by intensive study and to offering practical solutions.

The Western method consists of Problem Solving. Modern Science is still not convinced that not all problems can be solved by humans. With little consideration for the workings and efficiency of Nature, modern Science often turns a blind eye to the side-effects of its solutions. The application of pesticides is a case in point. Though pesticides can temporarily eliminate pests from agricultural lands, modern Science ignores the fatal diseases these pesticides can cause. We declare war on vermin like earthworms, without thinking how helpful they are. Can we call this attitude scientific or unscientific --- the attitude of exterminating creatures of every size that annoys humans so that only we and the creatures we need may survive?

How realistic is the billion-dollar researches that aim at the elimination of invisible microbes? There are countless microbes in Nature. Is it practicable to invent vaccines against every one of them? It has been decades since we started our fight against the visible mosquito. Yet, with unprecedented power, it has been infecting us with more and more novel diseases.

There is a folk tale in our village about a man who was scared to sleep on account of mosquitoes. He was a government employee. He was afraid of creatures such as mosquitoes and bumblebees. He would start to spread his mattress at seven in the evening. He would shake the bedspread for hours together and get into bed by about ten in the night. Right at that time, he would hear a mosquito humming. Instantly, he would get up and turn on the light. He would then see some insects around the light. Shooing them away, he would turn off the light. The humming would start again. Again, he would turn on the light - - - Thus, he would spend his nights without sleep.

We also follow the same practice. Earlier, we used to keep our body cleansed with spices and *Ayurvedic* oils and emulsions. To rid our houses and surroundings of dirt, we used to smoke frankincense and cultivate plants like basil and neem. Thus, without letting the pathological microbes invade us, we were able to defend ourselves against them. Instead of chasing away the mosquitoes, isn't it better to take precaution against their attack?

Rather than solving the problem, the oriental approach is to gain mastery over the problem so that we are not affected by it. In other words, the oriental approach emphasizes human coexistence with the problem. Modern Science and Technology has not succeeded in providing us a good life. As a result, the state of human mind and the state of environment are daily deteriorating. Conflicts and contaminations accumulate. We are robbed of joy; grief and grievances surge.

The system of education in ancient India never aimed only at material gains. '*Dharma*' was our custom in life. An awareness of *Dharma* ensured that even when our activities reap material gains, they do not harm us, or our fellow beings or Nature.

The only solution to our tragic situation is an appropriate harmony between Science and *Dharma*. We invaded Nature to achieve material gains blindly. The miseries we have invited for decades have turned our world uninhabitable. What is more saddening is the fact that we are repeatedly experimenting with the same system to solve these miseries. By means of decades of Western system of education, we have exiled from all areas a society with an awareness of *Dharma*. The administrative officials of education came into power because they got their degrees by giving the expected answers to the questions set by the government's bureaucracy bereft of creativity and thinking power. Under any kind of government, these officials will slavishly continue their western method. Our education is in the control of a mechanical group of people that is not even aware why they are there in the job. Today's westernized system of education mechanizes even the creative individuals in our society.

THE MECHANIZATION OF SOCIETY

The existing method of education is to transform society into efficient machines. Today, nearly all competitive exams are computer-based. The answers of these exams are also scanned by the computer, using Artificial Intelligence (AI). That means, a student can pass the exam with flying colors, if his answers are the same as the programmed ones. Do the student's creativity and thinking have any place in such a system? The successful candidate turns into a machine just like the computer. This method of education changes our brain into just a computer --- a system that feeds data into our memory and retrieves them when the need arises. The student is not even free to independently analyze these data. There is not much variation in the memory of students. Just as in the case of the computer, our memory and forgetfulness depend on the quantity of files stored in our memory. The difference between memory and forgetfulness is very little:

'Remembrance is the forgetting of unnecessary things; forgetting is the remembrance of unnecessary things.'

What matters in this context is the 'unnecessary things'. Those things depend on individual interests. But our Board of Education has snatched away this freedom.

Rather than exploring the possibilities of acknowledging and nurturing the unique individual talents, our Boards of Examination persuade our students to memorize their readymade questions and answers. Such a process serves only to kill the genius of our youth. Once, when I was teaching Heisenberg's 'uncertainty principle' to an Intermediate class at a private institution, one of the best students asked me after the class, "Why should I learn this? In what way will it be useful for me?" I explained to him its practicality as best as I could. Then he asked further, "Sir, do you think any of our students will be able to reach such a field? Then, why do you waste time and money to teach this to thousands of students?" I had only one answer in reply to him, "You need to have a degree to get a decent job, and it's the government's decree that you should study these sorts of topics. We need to answer the way they expect to the questions they prepare, if you need their certificate."

There have been attempts in many parts of the world to replace this mechanical system of education with alternative systems. Paulo Freire's 'Pedagogy of the Oppressed' is a significant work that influenced the people who were engaged in reforming education in the1970s. Freire was working with the indigent, illiterate farmers in Brazil. His experiments and analyses helped to create the awareness about the importance of education as a political process among the formally illiterate and the urgency of implementing it. His discoveries like the Cleansing of Conscience and Banking Education (the method of depositing knowledge in the learner) were thrilling. It was he who presented the difference between the Problem-Posing Education and the Banking Education.

By romanticizing the existing reality, Banking Education keeps concealed certain facts. This romanticizing conceals the fact how humans manage to survive in this world.

In the Problem-Posing Education, debates that expose reality are inevitable. While Banking Education considers learners to be dependents, Problem-Posing Education turns them into critical thinkers. The system like Banking Education sets aside intelligence and hides creativity. Thus, it rejects the biological and historical duty of developing a holistic human being.

In contrast, Problem-Posing Education, by virtue of creativity, reflects reality and functions accordingly. Humans achieve perfection only when they engage themselves in exploration and creative transformation. To put it briefly, the theory and application of Banking Education turns humans into a stagnant and impotent force, without considering them to be beings of great history. But the Problem-Posing method acknowledges the history of humans and takes that as its starting point to function.

There is an important reason for mentioning 'The Pedagogy of the Oppressed'. The method of Problem-Posing Education is in many ways similar to our ancient system of education. Of those similarities, 'the Study of Self' is one. Along with the study of the external world, a study of one's own self through introspection was a part of the ancient system of education. Also, this method had made it possible to discover one's talents and interests. As in the Problem-Posing education, it used to kindle motivation in the learners and answer their questions arising from that motivation. An examination of our *Upanishads* will bear this out. The '*Prashnopanishad*' in the *Atharvaveda* is in the form of a quiz. The '*Thalavakara Upanishad*' of the '*Samaveda*' and the '*Kenopanishad*' of the '*Brahmana*' are also good examples (The word 'kena' means 'by whom?' or 'by what?'). It is said that everything in this world exists either as the consumer or as the consumed. The objects of the senses are there for the consumption of the senses. The eye consumes forms and the ear the sounds. The '*Kenopanishd*' reveals the knowledge of Brahma as well as that of the senses. It has also allegories that lead one from egoism to self-awareness. In one of these allegories, in which the ego of the gods gets destroyed to create self-awareness, Brahma reveals himself in the guise of a Y*aksha* and teaches the gods what "I'" is, to make them realize their true self.

Modern education trains us to lose self-awareness and leads us to be arrogant. Every living creature learns from Nature what its self is and what its self is not. However, modern/western education destroys that skill of learning and nurtures egoism. Along with cultivating the pride of being a graduate, or a postgraduate, or an engineer, or a doctor or a scientist, modern education also spreads in the society the awareness that the formally illiterate are unintelligent. The inferiority and superiority complexes disseminated by the certificates from Boards of Examinations do great damage in our society. We have been suffering their evil consequences in all fields including that of agriculture. Spending billions of rupees, we launched the 'Green Revolution' to step up productivity in our agricultural lands where the farming had been traditional and inexpensive. The introduction of chemical pesticides and fertilizers, and high-yielding and non-reproductive seeds brought the control of the field of agriculture into the hands of the government. Traditional farming was almost eliminated. Farming became exorbitantly expensive and came into the control of the graduates of agriculture who knows not a thing about the soil, climate and cultivation. The farmers, who lived for decades harmoniously as a part of Nature and who loved farming became scarecrows. Hundreds of billions of rupees were spent from our tax-money to destroy this domain of traditional farming. And, what was the result? Deadly diseases like cancer and a generation with genetic defects. In the district of Kasaragod in Kerala, when people sprayed Endosulfan in defiance of Nature, what they reaped was a generation of deformities. The tragedy caused by some avaricious people is still being borne by a society that has long been fighting against poverty and misery - - - a society that is too weak to even protest against those who have shattered their hopes. But the people in power who triggered the tragedy still live without any kind of discomfort.

It is the western education In India that taught humans the arrogance that all natural resources are there for them to make monetary profit. When we defy Nature, it will react and turn violent. And, then natural calamities and disasters ensue.

When one does farming, there is a law of Nature involved in it. For example, take the farming of cashew (It was cashew-farming in Kasaragod). When the cashew blooms, a part of the flowers is for bees and other insects. These creatures help in pollination. But, refusing to give these creatures anything and declaring everything in the trees as ours, we, the avaricious kill them with deadly pesticides. Because the pests eat a small part of total flowers, we declare war on them with chemical weapon. We did flinch an inch in spending money for this war. When the flowers bear fruit, a part of the fruit is for birds and beasts. We send an army to destroy even them. For Nature, pests, birds, beasts, vermin and human are all its creatures. So when the species of humans appropriate everything without yielding to the others what they deserve, Nature gives them deadly diseases like cancer as a reaction. Yet, we learn nothing from that. Instead, we keep defying Nature, and Nature keeps unleashing natural calamities on us. To put in a nutshell, modern education provides us with more and more stupidities.

This is not a conflict between two systems of education but a conflict between two systems of philosophy --- between the oriental and the occidental philosophies. The philosophy of the West consists in conflict and elimination of the enemy. It considers all living thing only materialistically. It is vision that cannot comprehend what life in itself is. In contrast, the philosophy of the East is one of harmony. It views all the creations of universe as one. The difference can be observed in all areas.

THE SCENE OF AGRICULTURE

THE ORIENTAL APPROACH

Natural seeds and plants and natural pollinators like microorganisms and insects, all have a say in farming. They pollinate and fertilize the soil with their dung. Creatures like birds and squirrels also pollinate and eat fruits to which they are entitled. They leave their droppings in farming fields. Earthworms till the land. They leave not only their droppings in the soil but also their own body as manure. Thus, they help the soil to maintain its vitality. Plants receive sunlight. They take in carbon dioxide and release oxygen for us. Also, they receive rain and release it as vapor. When they die, we use them in the form of wood, or logs or some fossil fuel. How amazing is this state of balance in Nature - -- the state in which the sun, the earth, the birds, the beasts and the worms live in cooperation with one another! Here, there is no problem of food, or disease or garbage. Humans have only the role of a supporter in this process. Any role other than that of a supporter has not created anything worthwhile.

THE OCCIDENTAL APPROACH

Many of those who have had modern education will find it difficult to see how a philosophy that emphasizes only materialism affects life. It is a part of their belief that spirituality cannot go hand in hand with materialism. Western philosophy has only one aim - -- material gain. It believes that Nature is there only for humans and that humans can bring under control all natural phenomena. Western philosophy and modern stream of thought are often flawed because it believes that all creatures must live in accordance with human-made laws. We must realize the human limitations at the same time as we realize human possibilities.

In the system we call 'western method', or 'modern method' or 'scientific method' we often come across the question of 'scientific evidence'. What is it that we call 'scientific evidence'?

The term is used in the sense of that which convinces our senses of perception, mind and intellect. As mentioned earlier, we cannot discover the causes of the fundamental phenomena in Nature. However, we may be able to explain the 'how' of many of these phenomena. And, to be sure, we have made many discoveries on the basis of these explanations. It is impossible to find out why our hearts beat or why the earth goes round the sun. But we can explain how the heart beats. On account of the limitations of language, there has often been confusion in this regard. It is considerably arduous to find out the causes of fundamental natural phenomena. We, more often than not, mold our thoughts in keeping with the knowledge we have secured through our senses of perception. Strangely, we find it hard to accept the limitations of our senses. What I mean is that we cannot have a holistic view of reality, if we depend only on our senses.

One with jaundice sees everything as yellow. Some people are congenitally color-blind. One out of ten has color-blindness. Certain people cannot perceive a particular color and certain others cannot see more than one color. But many of these color-blind people are unaware of this fact. It is difficult to convince them that their sight is not perfect and that they should not believe their eyes.

Bernard Shaw was color-blind. But he realized his blindness only at the age of sixty. Someone gifted him a green suit on his sixtieth birthday. He went shopping to get a matching tie for the suit. What he bought was a yellow tie. When his secretary met him on the street, she asked him, "Sir, why are you wearing a yellow tie to go with your green suit?" Shaw replied, "Are you joking? Aren't the tie and the suit of the same color?" When the secretary said that she was serious, Shaw got his eye tested. That was when he discovered that he was color-blind. He was blind to the color, green.

We can't be very sure whether what we see is really real or whether things are really the way we see them. What we see is just our inference; we can only believe that what we see is real.

The capability of senses varies from individual to individual and from one living being to another. We cannot insist that only those things we perceive within the limit of our senses are real. A dog can hear what we cannot hear; it can smell what we cannot smell. It is because dogs can surmount the limitations of our senses that we form dog squads in the police and military forces to unearth evidence for us.

UNDERSTANDING THE POTENTIAL OF SENSES

Just as one must realize the limitations of the senses, one must also understand their potential. Let us have a look at the contributions of ancient India. The *Mahabharatha*, comprising more than one hundred thousand verses and over four thousand characters and involving all creatures of the universe, is a miraculous *magnum opus* composed in the style of magical realism. People of today even doubt whether it is possible for a human being to compose the *Mahabharatha*. It is something of a miracle for those who cannot write even a few verses after securing their post graduation by spending almost two decades in schools and colleges. It is against this background we should consider the potential of meditation. We are blind to our inner potential, as our senses are directed to the external world. We reject the findings and knowledge of ancient Indians. As we spend our time studying question bank and are not allowed to think anything else, we are not able to contribute geniuses to the world in these modern times like the ancient Indian geniuses. Yet we think that we are much more intellectually endowed than the geniuses of ancient India. Let us examine some of their discoveries. They are better and more perfect than those of the modern times. We have only distorted these findings in the name of innovation.

MUSIC

Once our 'divine singer', Yesudas on his visit to the Gulf countries performed songs in all kinds of languages including the Western and the Arabic. He said that our classical music, because it is comprehensive, is so flexible as to subsume all kinds of music. We cannot alter its seven notes into eight; nor can we reduce those notes to five. But do we remember those great pioneers who composed them or does anyone teach about them?

THE PERFORMING ARTS

Is there anywhere else in the world a systematic text of performing arts like the *Natyashasthhra* which contains a scientific systematization of various performing arts from various parts of India? Yet we do not learn anything about its author, *Bharatha Muni*. We do teach and present the *navarasas* (the nine emotional expressions) but we never give any thought either to their systematization or to the people who designed them. Kerala's indigenous forms of Art like *Kathakali, Koodiyattam, Ramanattam, Krishnanattam* and *Theyyam* are thousands of years old. After the birth of the state of Kerala, we started considering them Kerala's Art forms. Apart from presenting these forms of arts as items at the Youth Festivals, we never teach their history to anyone. The ingredients for *chutti* (the 3-D make up) in *Kathakali* are all natural. Only recently have the make-up companies brought into use the 3-D make-up. Though the world's excellent scientific forms of dance were popular in India thousands of years ago, we do not appreciate their glory and greatness. Our dance forms are miraculous aesthetic forms that combine Art, Music, Literature and Histrionics.

PAINTING, SCULPTING AND ARCHITECTURE

Our frescos are a wonder even today. They were done using absolutely unadulterated natural resources and, therefore, remained intact for centuries. Likewise, a visit to the ancient palaces and temples across India will reveal the glory of our art of sculpting. The *Taj Mahal*, one of the Seven Wonders of the World, and the ancient temples and beautiful palaces that remain without any damage even today are not only the pride of our country but also testimony to our ancient architecture. How many of the concrete and glass houses of modern days can rival these structures?

SCIENCE OF MEDICINE

It is in India that we find the oldest medical science of the world. There were many works like the *Charakasamhitha* and the *Sushruthasamhitha* in the field of medicine. These works were the result of centuries of observations and experimentations by our ancient seers. After some centuries, the western scientists hijacked many of these results, patented them and published them in their names. Take a look at the detailed description of pathogenic microbes in the *Charakasamhitha* of B.C. 3000:

"The various microbes are round, invisible, hirsute and cupreous in color; they maybe pathogenic or not." (*Charakasamhitha: Vimanasthanam*, 3000 B.C.)

There are so many such books of medicine in our India that deal with comprehensive physiology and all kinds of diseases and their treatments. But we never tried to study them or research into them. Also, the field of medicine is now completely ceded to Allopathy. Everything in the medical field including policy-making is in the hands of allopaths. There are many highly talented and experienced experts of *Ayurveda* in our country. The practice of *Ayurveda* was immensely popular in Kerala (before its formation as a separate state). Like *the Kottakkal Arya Vaidyashala* headed by Padmashree P.K. Varyar, there are many Houses of Medicine in Kerala, spearheaded by world-renowned *Ayurvedic* doctors. Many eminent people from across the world have come here to get treated and have left after complete recovery. It was the traditional doctors in the villages who had laid the foundation for the practice of health in Kerala. These non-profit making traditional doctors were the repositories of practical training based on the folk-wisdom of many generations. And, there is an urgent need to encourage and nurture this wisdom.

A large batch of scientists including one of my friends in the University of Toyo of Japan is researching the nano-particles in gold, *brahmi*, *vayambu* and the like. They are trying to find out how these particles enable the enhancement of intelligence. Today, our herbal medicines are cultivated and researched in countries like Japan and Germany.

THE QUALITIES OF DOCTORS

The qualities a doctor has to have are recorded there in *Charakasamhitha*. These are: i) Affability toward everyone ii) Compassion for the patient iii) Reverence for the practice of medicine and iv) A philosophical approach towards all living and non-living being. Just as in the field of Allopathy, there are also graduates in the field of *Ayurveda*. But they too follow the policies and systems of examinations devised by the allopathic doctors. We often find them rejecting and humiliating the traditional apothecaries, instead of acquiring knowledge from them. However, one can easily see on a closer examination that the best doctors and hospitals are those that follow the traditional system. In these hospitals, we can see masters who have traditionally been trained. It is in search of these masters that the various world-leaders arrive at the Houses of Medicine. If we can appropriately coordinate these traditional doctors and their folk wisdom, we can revolutionize our field of medicine. It will be great injustice to the coming generation and to the world at large, if we destroy this wealth of folk wisdom and experience.

The traditional doctors were the only ones on whom the country folks could depend. But, today, they are branded as 'quacks'. Without even bothering to look into their traditional knowledge, people tarnish them in public, isolate them and even imprison them when an opportunity arises. A huge industrial lobby is growing on the strength of the trust that *Ayurveda* has acquired through the traditional system of medicine. Like the study of Allopathy, the study of *Ayurveda* is reduced to a four-year- degree course. Today, they have changed *Ayurveda* into a system modeled on Allopathy by prescribing instant herbal tinctures and medicines for diseases. The genuine method of *Ayurveda* is not to treat the disease or its symptoms but the patient. In that method, if the same symptoms of a disease are found in two different patients, the treatment will be different for those patients.

A few months back, along with an allopathic doctor, I had the fortune to visit the *Kottakkal Arya Vaidyashla* and meet P. K. Varyar. We asked him about his daily routine. He said that he would retire to bed early and get up early in the morning. After refreshing himself, he would light the lamp in memory of his uncle. Then he would pray and meditate. Every day he would recite a chapter of *Ashtangahrudaya.* My friend asked him the reason for reciting *Ashtangahrudaya.* His reply was worth meditating upon. He said, "Our system is totally different from that of Allopathy. You prescribe medicine for the disease and its symptoms. The lab technician tells you what the disease is and the medical representative tells you what the medicine is. You can treat patient by coordinating these two. Besides, you can use life-long the medical degree you have acquired. In our system, we treat the patient. We have to accurately study the nature of each patient separately. We can't treat them on the strength of a degree we got in the past. Hence, we have to study every day." Then he posed a question: "How many allopathic doctors of my age (He is 97 years old) are doing practice?" Even today he treats free a definite number of patients.

Many traditional Houses of Medicine which had served as the backbone of our medical field have been locked down on the strength of government laws. The new generation has moved on in search of alternative jobs. I would like to make a request to the *Ayurvedic* doctors including the BAMS graduates: Please don't laugh at the traditional doctors who were the backbone of *Ayurveda* as 'quacks'; instead, treat them as your masters and learn from the method and insights they have acquired. You can learn from them how to treat the patient rather than the disease. The government has to come forward to set up a system to preserve their traditional knowledge and its application. Years ago, it was reported in the media that the late Shivaraman Vaidyar, a native of Kozhikode, had found a remedy for rabies and had to fight for 32 years to get it patented. However, nothing was heard about it later. The man who had almost no support and who sacrificed his whole life to discover the medicine had to wage a battle for over three decades to get it patented. Still, the modern medicine-lobby forbids the release of the medicine into the market. During these three and a half decades innumerable people have died of rabies. The modern-lobby doesn't want to encourage the use of that medicine to solve the problem. They just want to garner profit. The irony is that the synthetic drugs made after experiments costing billions of dollars get patented and released into the market within a brief span of time. This lobby has totally vanquished the field of medicine and turned into the biggest profit-making industry in the world.

YOGA AND MARTIAL ARTS

In ancient India, what was practiced was building immunity to diseases. The secret of our health lay in balanced diet and physical training. It is a matter of great relief that the world has now recognized our system of Yoga. Today, Yoga is a part of school syllabus in many parts of the world. But, whether our country has given it due consideration is a matter to be investigated. Martial arts like '*kalari*' were once a part of our daily routine. We had also centers for *kalari* treatment and physiotherapy.

Once I took a friend of mine to a centre for *kalari* treatment on his insistence, when he got his femur fractured. The master at the centre examined him and gave instructions to his assistants. He got a boat for massaging filled with medicinal oil and laid the patient with the fractured bone in it. Slowly, the master and his helpers started to massage the patient. In the midst of massaging they suddenly pressed the fractured femur into the right position, set it in splints and secured it with a bandage soaked in herbal medicine. I asked him about this treatment without the help of any X-ray, or painkillers or anesthesia. I found his answer logically sound. He said: "The X-ray will give us only a rough idea about the broken bone; it will not help us bandage it. We can bandage it, only if we feel the femur with our fingers." Then he added, "We keep massaging and changing the bandage on alternate days so that we can understand whether the bones are getting set in the appropriate way. At that time I remembered the experience of an expert orthopedic surgeon who set a fractured hand in a plaster cast after taking its X-ray. After twenty one days, when the cast was removed it was found that the bones were wrongly joined. It took twenty one days for the doctor to find out that the bones were set to join in the wrong way! The hand had to be again operated upon and put in a plaster cast.

The *kalari* master had something more to say about anesthesia and painkillers, "See, pain is a symptom of the disease. The diagnosis also depends on the location and nature of the pain. If you sedate the patient with painkillers, we cannot accurately understand the symptoms. Anesthetizing a patient for a surgery is an entirely different matter. Giving him painkillers cannot be compared to that."

Such decades-old traditional institutions as the *Kalari* Center are in active operation even today because of the faith reposed in them by the people. It is imperative that they should be sustained and preserved.

To sum up, if we examine the contributions of ancient India in this way, we can see that we had maintained eminence in all kinds of fields including Mathematics, Chemistry and Astronomy.

FEARS, WARS AND EDUCATION

It is by propagating fear that Western Education System and its product, the modern lifestyle, rule over us. The system creates an order in which we cannot think or question anything that displeases the government. This system of education that incorporates into it unwholesome information promotes the preservation of values and interests that militate against the children.

Modern Education has succeeded in achieving its anarchic goal of creating unnecessary anxieties in the parents about their children. A majority of the parents have been indoctrinated to see high-rise buildings, expensive uniforms and exorbitant fees as signs of excellence in education. School-brands have become tools for bragging. What gets ignored in all this hullaballoo is the children's flair and interests. The teachers also get entangled in the parental anxieties and pressures. There are even such parents in our society as train their two-year-old children for interviews to gain admission to L. K.G. classes. They do not know how much boredom and pressure they are instilling in their children. This system of education turns a spirited and sapient child into a dull and dead one.

The existing syllabus neither encourage the student's great longing for self-discovery nor does it allow any space or time for that discovery. It has no room in it for recognizing the student's potential. Students are fed up with this system of 'Banking Education' which just stuffs them with the quantity of knowledge to be imparted every month and every year, without bothering about their individual gifts, skills and interests. By and large, when we deposit some amount of money, we anticipate an increase in that capital over a period of time, as interest accrues. However, in this system of Banking Education, we stand to lose even the capital as time passes. Through Universal Education, we are indeed inflicting on the children this kind of spiritless education designed by the government.

I had an opportunity to talk to a few teachers and students in a C.B. S. E Indian school abroad. While I was talking to the high school students, I mentioned a few items of news like, 'India has won the World Cup', and 'Their school has won the football match at the national level'. When I asked them which of those items gladdened them the most, they replied that the news, 'Tomorrow is a holiday for the school' was the news that pleased them most. Even the teachers confided in me that it was the most welcome news. Then I wondered: For whom do we run this system of education that a majority of the people find dull? Why do we continue this system of education feared and disliked by both the children and their parents?

Let us take a look at the kinds of apprehensions this system of education generates in the children and parents:

APPREHENSION 1

The first and foremost apprehension that grips a parent is whether he or she would be able to secure for his child the admission to the best Nursery School.

APPREHENSION 2

Next comes the fear whether his or her child will always be able to maintain the top status in exams from the Nursery classes onwards. It will be useful to find out how many of the children with top rank in the Nursery and with fluency in reciting nursery rhymes have achieved success in life.

APPREHENSION 3

The parent is apprehensive whether his or her ward may fall to lower ranks in the classes. He or she wants the child to maintain the top position in all the subjects from the First Standard onwards.

APPREHENSION 4

Then comes the fear whether his or her child may fail to get A+ grade in the Tenth Standard.

APPREHENSION 5

After the child passes the Tenth Standard, the parent is worried whether his child may fail to get admission to his or her preferred group of courses.

APPREHENSION 6

The fear of Entrance/Exit Exams:

Many of the terms we use are paradoxical. Take for instance, 'Entrance Exams'. These are the examinations conducted to select students to be admitted to courses of Higher Education and Technical Education. Aren't these examinations really 'Exit (Elimination) Exams'? If a State had 5000 seats for medical courses and 4000 applicants for them, there would be no need for an Entrance Exam. But if there are only 5000 seats and 50,000 applicants, there will have to be an examination to eliminate 45, 000 aspirants. So, isn't such an examination fit to be called an 'Exit Exam'? And, this examination is on top of several other boring examinations the students have taken from Class I to Class XII. Also, what student-skills do these examinations test? How flippant this system is! To ace these tests, students learn by rote previous years' questions and answers and get trained at high-priced coaching centers. If they top in the rank-list, they can secure admission to the courses at a lower fee. If they are lower in the list, they can get admissions under the 'management quota', paying millions of rupees. Students entitled to 'reservation' need not be at the top in the rank-list either. Once the examinations are passed, everyone gets the same certificates. Both the makers and the takers of the Entrance Examination know that the test is just a sham. This area of testing has grown into a huge inviolable industry.

A majority of students of Classes XI & XII and their guardians live in fear of the social apprehension that they may fail to get admissions to these entrance examinations. The news of students' committing suicide out of the fear of examinations is ample proof of the fact that this fear has grown bigger than even the fear of death. Fear is born when self-assurance is gone and, to have self-assurance, there must be self-awareness. Our self-confidence diminishes in proportion to our alienation from Nature. The only people without self-confidence and self-awareness are we who claim to be modern.

Some time back my friends and I had an opportunity to pay a visit to East Africa. We stayed for three days in the Masai Mara jungle, one of the largest forests in the world. Our safari was by the trucks of Departments of Tourism and Forest. The forest sprawls across an area of 900 hectares and is home to wild animals like lions, tigers, zebras and elephants. We can trek into the jungle for about 100 to 150 kilometers. Inside the jungle, there are resorts designed in harmony with the nature of the wild. A great number of forest-dwellers live in this jungle. When we saw little children of five years and six years grazing cattle in the wild, we felt pity for them in our (un)civilized mind. So we visited one of the villages of these forest inhabitants. The fee for entry into the village was ten euros. The forest dwellers have the right to claim it. Each village has a person entrusted with the responsibility of guiding the tourists. We were apprehensive about the language for communication with the people of the forest. But as we entered the village, our worries vanished. Mr. Sam, the man responsible for the village, welcomed us in fluent English. The young men in the aboriginal

The author with his family at a school for aboriginals in the Masai Mara Forest

dress explained to us everything in detail. First, some the young men in the group welcomed us with a dance. Sam told us in detail about these dancers. They were dispatched with arms into the interior of the jungle for a year. They can visit their village only in the day time on certain appointed days. They were sent to the forest after training in arms, martial arts and school education. Each of them would have to bring a lion to the village within a year. Only after that they would be accepted by the village and permitted to marry. We also queried about the cow herding boys who didn't go to school. Sam explained to us the reason for that: Those boys must first learn the language of the wild; knowing the forest is the most important thing; otherwise, they cannot either survive in the wild or attend school. Later, they would join the Christian Missionary schools in the forest, where they would be given new Christian names. It was in this way that Sam had got his name. His original name was something else.

Sam took us to forest school where he had studied. The school teaches subjects like English, Science, Mathematics and Constitution. We found that the learning there was orderly and systematic. We felt that students had self-discipline and the freedom to maintain their identity.

A classroom at the school for aboriginals

Every living species has an ecosystem in which it lives and to which it is accustomed. Those forest dwellers that live happily, enjoying the unadulterated air, water and natural resources of the forest are really fortunate. They are not forced to live away from the forest and starve in concrete jungle. Nobody has given them any title deed in the forest. The forest belongs to them just as it belongs to other living creatures. All the rites and rituals in the village are in harmony with Nature. Those who are interested in studying and working outside have the right to do so.

We also visited the most famous school in Nairobi, Kenya. The fee at the school on an average is 250, 000 Indian rupees. The school situated in an area of 30 acres has all the modern facilities. However, once we see how the students' freedom is curtailed and how the students are intimidated into discipline, we will realize how mechanized the school-life is.

We understand that a student of the forest school can surmount any uncertain situation in life. But those who emerge out of the mechanized modern schools turn out to be increasingly fearful and stand shell-shocked when a crisis occurs in their life. As one acquires degree after degree, one's fear also increases. From the nursery classes on wards, the training that modern education imparts to the children is a kind of 'Don't Do!' which more often than not goes against common sense and logic. Thus, our system of education nurtures a category of people apprehensive of doing anything and incapable of acting independently.

A friend of mine, an I.A.S. officer, left his job to start an educational institution. It failed to rise to the standard of his expectation. When I asked him about the reason for the failure, he said, "We, the I. A. S. officers, are apprehensive of making up our mind on our own; we need someone to give us orders; it is an old habit that dies hard." This assessment by this intelligent and sincere officer is to the point. He was of the opinion that anyone who gets out of this system of education, rebelling against it will find success in life.

Once fear grips our mind, we become helpless to do anything. For example, if we are asked to walk across a- 1ft x 100ft- plank on the ground, we can easily walk. But, if we are asked to walk across the same plank suspended between two adjacent buildings, we will not be able to walk. It is our diffidence and apprehensions that pull us back. A cat will easily walk across that plank because it believes in itself. People in the wild and people without formal degrees too have confidence in themselves. For instance, when a high-rise tower is being constructed, we can see the engineers giving instructions from the ground and the laborers toiling bravely at the top of the tower.

It is a common sight to see high officials physically fitter than laborers lose their aplomb as they gain higher education. It is also a usual sight to see them standing consternated when they have to face small or big predicaments in their day-to-day life.

APPREHENSION 7

The biggest fear transmitted by modern education is the fear of failure. It is the collective of parents and teachers that is responsible for spreading this fear among the students. There are just two possibilities when one takes an examination: One either passes or fails. The one ready to accept failure alone is eligible to take an examination; that one alone deserves success. One can achieve success through

A teacher at the school for aboriginals explains methods of education

productive efforts, only if one is ready to accept success and failure equally. Success in life does not mean grand success in any examination; on the contrary, it is achieving success by living a life of values. The belief that wealth is the only criterion of intelligence and achievement is simply idiotic. If you ask me who was a great genius between the great billionaire Steve Job and Shankaracharya, my answer will doubtlessly be: "Shankaracharya". The last words of Steve Job are worth remembering. He died of the cancer of the pancreas at the age of sixty five. The words he uttered at his death are sure to change our outlook on life. He said, "I have made great achievements in the world of business. I worked hard and also partied a little. In the end, I made a lot of money. Now, as I battle against death in my hospital bed, I review my life. I realize one thing: If I lose my hard-earned money with pride, I can regain it. But I cannot regain my healthy life. You can employ a driver to drive your car but you cannot employ anyone to take over your disease." Enumerating and confessing the senselessness of even smallest things in his life, he emphasized the importance of a healthy life over wealth. It was at the age of sixty five when he was battling for life in the hospital bed that Steve Job realized the sense and senselessness of life. In contrast, Shankaracharya's greatness lies in the fact that he understood this lesson even at a very young age and tried to teach it to the world.

APPREHENSION 8

Sacrificing the pleasant period of teenage, donating pots of money and overcoming the fear of failure, once the students again learn and pass the boring courses of their parents' choice from the institutions the parents have selected for them, the next fear makes its appearance: the fear whether they can acquire a job with a salary and perks of their expectation. Thus the mindless rat race continues with more examinations and interviews.

Even people who are fairly well-off hesitate to start an institution. The reason, again, is the fear of failure --- the fear that the capital will be lost, if the institution fails. If we want a venture to succeed, we must first be ready to accept failure. When we launch an institution, there are two possibilities: It may succeed or it may fail. If we learn from our failures, we can try again. If we aim at perfect success and then fail, it will be difficult for us to revive ourselves because of depression, blame from our family and society and the psychological tension from the failure. But, before we begin our venture, if we consider its total failure, prepare ourselves mentally to face blames and problems and think of solutions, our progress will never be hampered.

The main role in spreading this fear in society is played by our family, society and our dear ones. When we celebrate our small and big victories, we brush aside and disgrace a large number of people, branding them as 'failures'. When we facilitate a child for bagging A+ grade in all subjects, we banish the majority of the rest of the children, calling them 'losers'.

But, in my experience, I have seen many of those who were certified by the society and teachers failing in life and those who were branded as losers winning in life. By 'success in life' I don't mean accumulation of wealth but an ethically conscious personality who serves the family and society like a Good Samaritan. I myself have come across persons with excellent academic record who later became the acme of corruption. Can we consider a person a 'success in life', when he or she reaches the highest echelons in office by giving and taking a bribe? There is at the same time another side to the story. If we look around, we can see many real social activists. They are people who struggle to make both ends meet and have no higher academic qualifications --- those who were branded as 'losers', after their academic examinations but those who come to our aid in any matter at any time of the day or night. Not only do they not take a bribe, they do not charge for their services either. They cannot be seen anywhere in the frontline of leadership; they are not just visitors at places of tragedy; they have no motive other than sincere, selfless service.

Honoring only those who secure high marks in examination by means of learning by rote conveys yet another message: If we want to appreciate you, you must have either wealth or a position of prestige; it doesn't matter whether if you acquire it by foul or fair means. However, we have in our country big business empires run by great personalities of immaculate ethical values. They are the backbone and pride of our country. They do not work just for fame.

Our western education's objective is often economic gain. Hence, students who sacrifice their sleep to study hard also aim at positions of power and money. Naturally, in such a scenario, the concept of 'service' as a duty is ignored. As the higher echelons in offices turn corrupt and nepotic, a majority of officials take to any means to ingratiate their superiors. Sincere and honest people find it extremely difficult to survive in our system of bureaucracy.

APPREHENSION 9

Once one succeeds in struggling to get a job, the next fear is about one's superiors, as they have the authority to give orders to the subordinates. The superiors quite often turn their subordinates into scapegoats to save their image. The subordinates thus start living in fear as they have to bear their superior's misdeeds.

Once, when an honest official joined duty, he was given an envelope by the peon at the end of his first month in the office. When he asked the peon about the envelope, he told him that it was his share of bribe. The man refused to take the share. Later I heard that, before his official term was over, he killed himself unable to bear the pressure at his office. After one joins an office, whether one is a bribe-taker or not, one lives in fear. Fear of one's superiors, fear of disciplinary action, fear of rightly finishing the job in time, fear of errors in executing the job --- the list of fear goes on and on.

The collective conscience is of course against corruption. But, at the individual level, people are ready to compromise as and when the need arises; they encourage corruption directly or indirectly. Our system breeds law-breakers and creates a society of people living in fear of official authorities.

Many of our laws are enacted in such a way that those who react against corruption can be intimidated as law-breakers. Many of these laws are obsolete and have to be updated or repealed.

Various kinds of taxes and tax laws are to be reenacted in a transparent way so that the public can grasp and obey them. Take the term, 'Sales Tax' for instance. When a common man hears the term, he may assume that it is the tax to be paid by the seller. In fact, this tax must be called "Buyers' Tax". When a merchant asks customers whether they want the bill of sales for a taxed product, most of them say they don't want it. Here, the end-customer is the tax evader. But the ordinary end-customer is not usually aware of this evasion. The corruption we often notice is of the lowest level --- a bribe of Rs. 100 or Rs. 1000. And, there will be government measures against that kind of corruption. But, what measures are taken against scams of high scale involving billions? Most of the corrupt at the higher level roam freely and safely like gentlemen in society. People of higher positions, who have political or other support, deceive the public because they are powerful enough to instill fear in us. If a poor man steals a roll of bread to satisfy his hunger, we beat him to death, taking law into our hands. We blaze in ethical wrath. No one will speak anything against the act. The very next day, we will justify a scam of billions of rupees.

When there arose a vehement protest against *Nokku Kooli* (illegal extortion by organized labor unions in Kerala under which wages are paid to trade union activists for allowing people to load or unload belongings using their own labor), many of us expressed our moral anger. True, the practice of *Nokku Kooli* has to be discouraged. But was the protest against this corruption a sincere reaction? I express here an experience of mine: When I was college student, I was waiting at the *Palayam* bus stand in Kozhikode. Suddenly a decently clad man (The man's dress was indicative of his high official status.) near me swooned and fell down. The other gentlemen beside me had also witnessed the sight. But nobody moved. The man was foaming at his mouth. Since I was fairly engaged in student politics in those days, I was friends with a few loading/unloading workers. They were there in a corner at the bus stop. I informed them about the man. They rushed to him and took him to hospital. They told me not to accompany them, as they could handle the situation on their own. In the evening, when I enquired of them about the man, they told me that he has had a heart failure and was recuperating in the I. C. U of the Medical College. What I mean to say is that these loading/unloading workers are the guards in our public places. They often return lost property honestly to its rightful owner. Maybe, they look rough in their appearance, lack formal education and dress themselves in shabby clothes. But their hearts are pure, maybe, because of their lack of formal education. We have become a society of people who rage against the corruption at the lowest level and keep quiet about the corruption at the highest level. The corruption we have to fight against is the corruption at the high levels.

APPREHENSION 10

The moment one joins one starts shouldering responsibilities. And, as one earns money, one starts facing new competitions. Most often, the job one gets is not the job one likes. The job one takes up is likely to be a job one hates. This is what Confucius had to say about getting a job:

"If you get a job you like, you never work even a single day; but if you get a job you hate, your life will only be stunted."

As one earns money, one starts competing for excellence in one's job and for getting promotion. There is also social competition: the competition to build better houses and facilities of life than the neighbors. This brings in its wake the fear of failure again. Apart from that, there will also be the fear of ill-health due to the physical and psychological pressure from these competitions. The fear-mongering advertisements by hospitals and insurance companies instill fear in us even in our intervals of entertainment. The health tips dished out by the social media to enlighten us are also threatening. Even when we have not so serious a disease, we are told that there are deadly symptoms. Thus, we are frightened into going through various tests and diagnoses. Eventually, we become life-long patients and pass away in hospital. The number of such patients is on the increase. Medical insurance and medical checkups survive on our fear. Deaths due to medicines are increasing in the world. The multi-storied hospitals that burgeon everyday are the indexes of our fear of death. Living in constant fear, unable to be among our near and dear and unable to get the last drops of water, we eventually die amidst the machines in the hospital. Once the machines confirm our death, the doctors duly declare it. They would say, 'Sorry.' Does that 'sorry' have the same sense as that of the 'sorry' that someone usually says? Thus, the fear that began even before we joined the nursery classes finds it end as the doctors say, 'sorry'.

THE WARS FEARS BREED

Living beings turn aggressive when apprehensions mount. An enemy is born when fear germinates in the mind. We fear those that can threaten us. When the enemy is stronger than us, we fight tooth and nail.

COMPETITION AND HOSTILITY

The foremost flaw of the system of western education is its practice of pitching students of diverse talents against one another. Each student has his own indigenous tendencies and talents. Any student of creative skills, thinking and ability to respond would find the imposition of a dull and dead syllabus in toto, in place of nurturing his or her innate tendencies. In such a situation, it would come as no surprise when intelligent students turn rebellious. They drift away from the mainstream of society and, as a result, society suffers from brain drain. Competition breeds hostility in students. It is necessary that the spirit of completion must be channelized into competition with oneself. Let the students compete with their own selves. Each individual in this world is incomparable. What is the use of a painter, a singer and an athlete competing with each other? When one vies with oneself, one improves day after day. One's skill-set enhances every day. But our education today is incapable of developing individual talents. Education must be able to guide the students to develop their inborn capabilities so that they can flourish in the area of their natural interest. When the completion with one's classmate is no more there, the hostility one feels will automatically vanish.

The very basis of occidental system is fear and hate, its ultimate end being monetary gain. As soon as a baby is born, it gets 'injected' with fear and war. To prevent diseases like polio, an army of fighters in the form of vaccines are injected into its body. Even the doctors who administer these vaccines have no idea about them. Polio vaccine is administered in the name of the fear that existed long back when a small minority was afflicted with polio. According to experienced and socially committed doctors like *Padmavibhooshan* Dr. B. M. Hegde, over 90% of the medicines in the market are unnecessary and causative of side-effects. Most of the allopathic medicines contain pesticides (antibiotics). The world has been suffering from the fallout of chemical pesticides and many countries have banned their use. Still, there is no measure against the use of antibiotics in human bodies. Whether it be in the field of medicine or in the field of agriculture, the western method is to wage war against the microorganisms. On the contrary, the method in the East is to build immunity to prevent the microbes' growth in our body.

Even after international health organizations have accepted the principle that food is the only medicine for any disease, the manufacturing and distribution of chemicals as medicine go on world-wide. In the eastern systems of medicine, including *Ayurveda*, medicines are manufactured from edible organic matter. When synthetic (chemical) medicines are consumed, several side-effects are produced. Hence, allopathic system gives us several of these effects. Even in this age, when the very theory of germs is being questioned, the chemical wars in our bodies against microbes are increasing day by day.

In the past, the battles were between warriors. Today, using the weapons we promulgate to be the achievement of modernity, we kill and deform innocent children and even generations. Aren't we moderns responsible for turning the whole world into a war filed by filling our society with panic? The system of modern education and its byproducts are pushing us into the tragedy of hurtling the world blindly into a competition the only aim of which is money and ephemeral comforts and conveniences.

We have been turned into 'Sisyphuses', as the Oriental Philosophy's backbone, ethical sense, was extirpated from our society. It is our folly that the myth of Sisyphus essentially reveals: Roll a gigantic boulder up the hill and, then, roll it down the hill and, again, roll it uphill. First, manufacture chemical fertilizers and pesticide by spending millions and use them widely in agricultural fields; eliminate creatures like earthworms from the soil; substitute the eliminated earthworms with earthworm-compost; produce nutrient-less, garbage-like food and breed cancer; then, get treatment for cancer by spending billions. When a large chunk of population becomes ill for decades, ask them to practice organic farming. In the name of white revolution, breed hybrid cows by spending millions and, afterwards, give them up in the name of low-quality and return to breed country cows --- There is no difference between Sisyphus and us.

Subsidize and help to burgeon factories manufacturing products like plastic, polythene and polyester which are easy to use but detrimental to Nature and ban them after decades --- the system of modern education has taught us that these kinds of reforms are right and that the traditional systems are unscientific. The surprising thing is that the people who teach us these things authoritatively and design the textbooks are those who have never done any farming.

ACHIEVEMENTS IN THE FIELD OF HEALTH/HOSPITALS

The organizations in the field of health claim that modern science has succeeded in providing the best health facilities and in eradicating many diseases like polio, cholera, leprosy and tuberculosis. Let us have a look into this claim by the health organizations.

FROM *JEEVANTONE* TO *SLIMLINE*

A few decades back, the health tonic, '*Jeevantone*' was widely advertised in newspapers. The advertisement displayed an emaciated man's photo, captioned 'before consuming *Jeevantone*' and another photo of a robust man, captioned 'after consuming '*Jeevantone*'. *Jeevantone* was widely available in those days.

But the advertisements we see today are those of products like '*Slimline*'. These advertisement show the picture of a fatty with the caption, 'before use' and the picture of a slim figure with the caption, 'after use'. This signifies one thing: If malnutrition was the problem in the past, today the problem is obesity. Earlier, it was diseases born of poverty like cholera and tuberculosis that were prevalent in our country. Today the diseases we face are because of over-nutrition. The diseases born of poverty are replaced by widespread diseases born of wealth like cholesterol, blood pressure, diabetes and cancer. Heavy use of chemical fertilizers to step up the soil productivity also served as a catalyst in this situation. Health organizations have nothing to say about the diseases born of wealth. Besides, billions of rupees are still being spent on deliberately vaccinating people against the diseases that they claim to have eradicated. They never tell the public about their side-effects.

THE IMPERATIVE FOR A HEALTHY SOCIETY

Our health organizations, political parties and the government believe that the excellence of the system of health lies in state-of-the-art hospital facilities.

Once, when a friend of mine, an ex-minister, was about to inaugurate a hospital, I asked him what he would say in his speech. He said, "I will say, 'May the hospital grow to greater heights with better and better facilities'." Then he turned to me and asked, "I know whenever you ask something, there will always be a catch in it; what would you wish them in this kind of situation?" I said, "My answer is simple. I will say, 'May this hospital be shut down very soon'."

Wishing a hospital to flourish is, in fact, wishing to have more and more patients in the land. In my opinion, a healthy society is a society without doctors, patients and hospitals.

But what organizations including WHO envision is a society of more doctors rather than a society without patients. Today there are huge lobbies of vested interests in the world involving the industries of medicine, medical equipment and medical education. They rule over the field of health all over the world by means of their power and pelf. They have silenced the voice against them by fettering our life, health and even thoughts. They say nothing about the increasing medicinal deaths in the world. In these times of 'Corona', we have seen in the western world the tragic result of the widespread growth of private hospitals and medical insurance. These lobbies are also tightening their grip in India.

Even doctors are now coming forward to enlighten us against these internationally spreading medical lobbies. In Israel, when the doctors went on a strike, the death-rate decreased after six months and the undertakers found themselves in trouble. Dr. Hegde has revealed that this incident was reported even in the British Medical Journal. Hegde, who is also an eminent cardiologist, also tells us that the disease called 'heart attack' is mainly a means of business. He reveals that even diseases like diabetes and cancer are nothing but a means of large-scale businesses. Regular medical checkups and free medical treatments are only ways of recruiting of patients into hospitals. As in the case of other living creatures, most of our diseases get cured on their own. Our body has a self-repairing system in it. What do we do when our bone is broken? We set it right and bandage it or set it in a cast. In three or four weeks, the bone will be set and the bandage or the cast can be removed. In 90% of self-curing diseases, symptoms like pain will also disappear, as the disease cures itself. But what do we do? We treat the symptoms with synthetic medicines. The treatment results in side-effects and causes new diseases. In the name of 'Free Medical Camps' what is being run is the process of turning patients with mild symptoms into lifelong patients. What is being sold there is the fear of all fears, the fear of death. Innumerable people have become patients in this way.

The system of *Ayurveda* was powerfully prevalent in various parts of India including Kerala. Some of the practices in *Ayurveda* were there in our food style, lifestyle and even in our rituals. Many medicinal herbs were a part of our daily life. Things such as turmeric, pepper, basil, onion and garlic were the very basis of our heath. But, today, when hospitals are considered to be the signs of health, Kerala has become the largest market for synthetic medicines. We don't even have the commonsense to realize that hospitals are not a sign of health but a sign of ill-health and unhealthy people.

In the past, every village had traditional doctors practicing at home. They would cultivate herbs at home and treat people. They used to receive as fee for their service whatever the patients gave gracefully as donation. It was these doctors who protected us by keeping us free from diseases. However, as the industry of medical degrees dominated the field of health and the number of people who bought these degrees spending millions of rupees increased, the field of health came completely under the power of money. Besides, exterminating the traditional lore of medicine and creating a society of people without immunity with the use of governmental authority, the vested interests began to produce patients. If we give a fraction of the millions we spend on hospitals to buy the products of those who do natural farming and encourage organic farming, we can save at least the coming generations.

We need to put into practice the principle that 'prevention is better than cure'. Corona virus has taught the world that the only defense against disease is immunity. We need to think over our options. Do we need clean air, water and food? Or, do we need medicines, hospitals and a society of people of ill-health?

HEALTH AND URBANIZATION

The trend of urbanization has been spreading for the last few decades in farming countries including India. It is imperative that this trend that distresses our life should be arrested. This is all the more relevant in these times of 'Corona'. Multi-storey skyscrapers are burgeoning aggressively in 'smart cities'. A western consumer culture has taken roots deeply in our midst, as a result of western culture and fashion. Today, we don't consider a habitat as inhabitable if there is only clean air, water and food. We now consider a place inhabitable only if we have near us hospitals, shopping malls and only if can order 'junk food' online. We don't have any worry about the pollution of land and air created by the density of population, the unclean water delivered in tankers, the formalin-contaminated fish preserved in freezers and vegetables laced with pesticides. Above all, we sacrifice our life for bragging that we are fashionable urbanites and not country bumpkins.

THE 'DISPOSABLE' CULTURE

I once participated in a three-day-academic workshop in I.G. N.O.U. conducted to discuss the present and future courses of study. All the vessels used there in all the three days were 'disposable' ones. Ironically, one of the courses we discussed was 'Waste Management'. You produce disposable material freely and cause tons of waste and, then, spends billions to learn waste management!

The concept of 'disposable' is a kind of culture --- one that is entirely western. The principle behind it is 'use and throw'. This 'disposable' culture has infiltrated into all the spheres, including the sphere of family relationships. Accumulation of waste, divorces, old-age homes and orphanages are all parts of this 'disposable' culture. This culture can be seen even in our construction and furnishing works. Our ancient buildings and temples are a hundred or thousand years old. Constructed by eminent architects, they still stand with splendor. Can any of the government buildings rival these edifices? The ancient architects were naturally gifted. But, today, the plans and estimates are prepared and approved by civil engineers of the Department of Public Works. These engineers got into B. Tech courses through entrance examinations and later came into power passing P. S. C. tests by rote-learning at a coaching centre the answers to its dead questions. How can we expect creativity and aesthetic sense from these authorities? I am not writing this to demean the existing engineers. The mechanism in operation involves engineers and contractors who mechanically mix cement and put up buildings. Many of the government buildings, within five years of their construction, start leaking and turn into ghost houses. Neither the misters of the government nor the bureaucrats are aware of the safety and soundness of the buildings. Also, these buildings cost billions of rupees. These '*Panchavadi Paalamas*' (flimsy structures), which are there to be inaugurated and then modified, are also the contribution of 'use and throw' culture created by the system modern education.

WHAT COVID-19 TEACHES

Humanity is passing through extraordinary times. For months, an invisible microorganism has laid flat the ignorantly arrogant humans who considered themselves invincible because of the growth in science and technology. Covid-19 has taught us the most important lesson that we are nothing before Nature.

In these days of Covid-19, what is the message conveyed by dense population, colossal waste and sky high concrete jungles? It was in the metros that Covid-19 ran rampant. In India, it was in cities like Mumbai and Delhi that Covid-19 was widespread. Covid-19 reminds us that it is high time that we checked the blind imitation of western models.

WE NEED 'SMART VILLAGES'

A glorious country like India must present to the world a model of development that renders life harmonious and comfortable for Nature, humans and coming generations. To that end what we need to establish is the model of 'smart villages', not 'smart cities'. Our governments must seriously consider whether we need such disasters as 'smart cities' that cost trillions of rupees. The tendency of people migrating en mass to big cities has to be checked. We have so many people who have given up their houses and farmsteads in the countryside to live in the cramped spaces of urban apartments. To bring in a change in this culture we need to develop well planned 'smart villages'. With meticulous planning, the activities of realty can be channelized into the project of 'smart villages'. The funds needed for creating a 'smart city' can easily help build a thousand 'smart villages'. These villages must be designed keeping in mind their natural resources, employment heritage, cultural heritage and farming heritage and the like. Efforts should be made to sustain the extinct and existing traditional occupations and culture. The method of school education and the syllabus must be radically transformed. The method of western education must be simplified and a simple syllabus must be made available universally to students. As it is done in many international systems of examinations, a simple curriculum can be there for the 'core system'. And, if a student wants to study in depth, he or she can be provided with the facility of 'extended option'. Of the total syllabus, one-third must help students to prepare for the examinations, another one-third to learn local culture and skills in local vocations and yet another one-third to gain mastery in some technology of their interest.

As in the mode of 'Technology-Enabled Community Schools', a syllabus incorporating both national and local elements has to be designed. The timetable has to be set in keeping with local circumstances. Each village must have an academic committee involving educational activists, eminent people in the field of Art and Culture and people of traditional, technological and practical knowledge. The transparency of this system can be enhanced if we also include a social auditing system that comprises parents, experts in various fields and village representatives.

'Technology-Enabled Community Schools' are schools capable of effectively conveying to the villages the technologies developing globally and of nurturing professionals in this field. To make it practicable, small units of these schools can be set up with the help of I.T. companies. Also, those who are experts in the field can be employed there. Today, most I. T. companies prefer 'work-at- home' and a majority of the employees are people who migrated to cities from villages. If these people can work at home in their villages, they can not only escape from the cost of urban living but also make better gains from a small-scale salary.

INFORMATION TECHNOLOGY AND ARTIFICIAL INTELLIGENCE

Even at present, we have not given enough importance to subjects like Information Technology (I. T.) and Artificial Intelligence (A. I.). It is teachers with degree and B. Ed. in other subjects who teach these subjects in school. They often teach them uninterestedly under duress. If a village has an I. T. establishment, students can be trained in these subjects by the technological experts from that institution. Besides, we have now many online trainings and mobile applications. Digital contents are available even for science-subjects. Utilizing the potentials of these technological aids, our schools must become technology-enabled learning centers. Also, eminent people from the field of Art, Music, Dance, History and Literature can be invited as guest teachers to train students interested in such subjects. Many nations whose mother tongue and first language is English provide globally the facility for getting trained in a foreign language; for example, English which has grown today into an international language (the tests conducted at various levels by Cambridge International Examination [C. I. E.]). Students can avail themselves of these tests. If a student passes Cambridge Diploma Exam, it can be included in his or her Tenth Standard mark list and regarded as a topic of English. When does a Microsoft Office (Ms Office) certificate gain professional value --- when it is given by Microsoft or when it is given by our government? If a student secures Ms Office certificate, our government must include it as a subject in his or her Tenth Standard certificate. It is to be seen how the existing bureaucrats functioning comfortably in the established system of education and conservative teachers would receive these changes. So, the government has to parallely experiment these innovations without changing considerably the syllabus and 'chalk & talk" system. It is rather practically difficult to change an existing system radically. For instance, when we attempt to reform big cities, there will be resistances. Then, we create 'satellite cities' --- just as New Delhi was created when Old Delhi had to be modified. So, it is practically easy to develop a parallel educational system without attempting to reform the existing one.

Disasters often stem from flaws of conceptions of 'I', 'Me' and 'Mine'. It is absolute foolishness when we turn selfish, giving up the idea that our welfare is guaranteed by the welfare of others.

We always scream at the top of our voice for changes. Not even a single fundamental phenomenon of Nature can we change. Humans, who are a part of Nature, must live in accordance with the laws of Nature. We can make our children obey in two ways --- with love and with fear; in other words, by means of 'carrot and stick' policy. When we make them obey with love, we have to consider their interests; but when we use fear, those interests can be ignored. The eastern approach to Nature is that of affection and the western approach is that of intimidation. Nature responds in both cases correspondingly. The system of education in villages must be that of affection towards Nature. It should impart the self awareness that we are a part of Nature. Training in meditation has to be an integral part of the syllabus.

When I once visited Maharshi Mahesh University in America, I had the opportunity to speak on *Dharma* and Science. The people at the University give great importance to meditation in their studies. The University sprawling over 400 acres has spacious meditation halls. It is the time for silent meditation from 8.30 to 9.30 in the morning. One has to enter the hall after removing one's footwear very far away from the hall. The silent meditation happens in a theater. Students and teachers enter the theater silently and sit in silent meditation from 8.30 A.M. to 9.30 A. M. I too participated in this meditation. The experience was a special feeling.

It is after this meditation that students enter their classes. The self-discipline of the students with concentrated and collected minds entering the class is surprising. The Uni-

The author at the Meditation Centre of Maharshi Mahesh University in America

versity has students even from India and Pakistan. When many other universities have become centers of anarchy and pubs and night life have become an inalienable part of student-life, these kinds of universities are the only hope of parents. '*Annapoorna*', the mess-hall in this University, is almost wholly vegetarian.

Meditation develops one's self-awareness and helps discover one's innate abilities and guides one towards profound levels of thinking. The wonderful works of seers like *Valmiki* were the result of uninterrupted meditation. Behind all small and big discoveries lies a meditative mind. Even Stephen Hawking, who died recently, had really a meditative mind.

There is a need for developing a meditative mind in children to aid them in thinking and to instill in them an ethical sense. They should have the awareness that none of their activities would harm Nature in any way. So, at least one-third of their formal education should be dedicated to activities in harmony with nature, like farming and cow-rearing. Generally, we ridicule people who make essential things for us. So parents may not like their children involving in agriculture. The sense of 'dignity' also has a part to play in this. To solve this problem, people belonging to fields like I. T. should, therefore, spend some definite time for these activities with the students. Each village must be a center of 'start-ups' as per its potential and should become self-sufficient. Everyone including the traditional workers and technological experts of the village must be a part of the project. We have divided jobs into 'white collar jobs' and 'blue collar jobs'. This division has to be cast away. In many areas it has been discarded. For example, running a barbershop was considered a blue collar job earlier. When the barbershop became a beauty salon and the barber a beautician, the job became a skilled white collar one. The same is the story of the cook who became 'chef'.

Each student must have the opportunity to professionalize his or her individual talent. If technological experts grow up by interacting with Nature, gaining physical training and practical training, they will execute their duty with self-confidence and gumption. Then, instead of the aforementioned engineers who give instruction from the ground, there will be engineers who would be bold enough to work atop buildings. Our productivity will increase many fold, if we can develop a society of people who enjoy the job they do.

The author with the University authorities

The expertise of people like teachers and I. T. experts must be utilized for half of the jobs in 'smart villages', like agriculture and the processing of agricultural produce. Let our village be excellent and beautiful in all fields such as education, culture, health and employability. Our mission must be to revive the pristine rurality of the village and not the urbanization of the village. The village must find the solution to almost all of its problems in the village itself.

India was the leading light to the world in ancient times. It is inevitable that it should win that position back.

UNLEARNING
[QUESTIONS WE SHOULD ASK OURSELVES]

'Brutal' is the term we use when we see heinous acts. What we mean by this is that we are civilized and brutes, animals are not. When we compare ourselves with beasts, we will realize that there are certain common qualities. If we examine them, we can understand in whom lies the 'brutality' --- in the brutes or in us?

1.FOOD --- WHAT, WHEN AND HOW MUCH?

If we observe a lion, we can see that it goes after game only when it is hungry. After catching its quarry, it eats only that much which is necessary to satisfy its hunger. The rest of the prey will be left in the forests for other animals to have. If you let out a puppy and a calf, the puppy will eat bones and the calf will eat grass. No animal will eat food, once their hunger is sated. No cow is ever bored eating grass every day.

Humans eat as much as they can and keep the rest of the food in refrigerators. They will consume this for days to come. They will keep the meat of the animals for consumption in the freezer for weeks or months. When it goes bad, they will just throw it away without giving it to any animal.

If you let out a human child, like the calf and the puppy, it will eat anything and everything. It will eat even after its hunger is sated. To top it all, it will eat even an ice-cream.

A cow or an elephant never finds boring the same food it gets daily. But we get easily fed up with the same food, if we have to have it for two days in succession. We are always in search of 'variety' food every time. Like foxes, humans live in the night overfeeding themselves and sleep till it is noon next day.

2.SLEEP

Both humans and animals sleep. Beasts and birds, following their nature, sleep and wake up exactly at the same hour. Crows retire to bed before sunset and wake up at dawn. We used to know that it was sunrise when the rooster crowed. No diurnal animal will eat or go foraging after sunset. They don't need an alarm-clock to get up in the morning. No rooster would apologize for oversleeping and crow at noon.

In contrast, we don't know when and where to sleep. We sleep in buses, offices and schools. We sit till late into the night at a restaurant or in a theatre or before the TV and, later, take sleeping pills to invite sleep. Sleep is a boon from nature. There are beautiful descriptions about sleep in our *Upanishads*. William Shakespeare in his famous 'Macbeth' says about sleep,

> "Macbeth does murder sleep,
> the innocent sleep,
> sleep that knits up the ravell'd sleeve of care,
> the death of each day's life,
> sore labour's bath,
> balm of hurt minds,
> great Nature's second course,
> chief nourisher in life's feast."

There are many instances about sleep in this play. A good sleep is the sign of a mind at ease. There are people who are put up at five-star hotels but remain sleepless even after taking sleeping pills. At the same time, there are also many destitute people who sleep soundly on pavements of roads. Sleep is a phenomenon that every living thing practices regularly. Every one of them follows it systematically. The only living species that is insincere in sleep is the humankind.

3.FEAR

Every living creature has fear. Any animal has a natural ability for escaping from its enemies: Deer has its running skill; some animals can fight with their tooth and nail; birds can fly; some creatures can spew venom; some others are capable of escaping their enemies by means their physical strength. When a dog or a cat is asleep, it knows how to escape if a poisonous snake approaches it. It can identify its enemies. When it climbs a tree or leap from tree to tree, it is aware of its ability. It knows what and when it should fear. It never lives in fear all its life. But humans are the only creatures that do not know what and when they should fear. We live in great many fears: Will there be a decline in the value of shares in the Stock Market? Where is the price of gold heading to? Will the interest on mortgage escalate? Is my headache a symptom of some mortal disease? Will my son be able to secure a top rank in the Entrance Examination? The list of fears is unending. And, all these fears are not in our control. When we are engrossed in reading the Stock Exchange news about the market status, we will not even be aware if a snake bites us. Without knowing what to be afraid of and when to be afraid, a majority of us, humans, live in needless fear all our life and die of some disease. The only creatures that commit suicide are humans and it is fear that triggers suicide. Thus, even in the case of fear, animals have more practical sense than humans.

4.SEXUALITY

A couple of years ago, I had a chance to participate in a debate over human violence and sexual offense. One of the participants in the debate was of the opinion that sexual violence and murders were caused by women's dressing style. In my reply, I said that if that was the case, rape must be quite common in dense forests. The beasts we call 'cruel' walk nude in the forest. All animals possess sexual instinct and it operates according to a law of Nature. That is why a lioness or a cow-elephant does not get subjected to a gang-rape. The daily gang-rapes and murders we hear about happen only among humans. Even our domestic animals are decent. Even they follow the laws of Nature.

In all the aforementioned basic thing, who emerges as decent --- the humans or the beasts? Just as calling the 'buyers tax' 'sales tax' and 'exit exam' 'entrance exam', the term 'brutal' is paradoxical. Maybe, we can use this term till animals learn language. I remember a verse by Kunjunni Master:

"Why do you engage in skirmishes, dogs,
as though you were humans?"

A SOCIETY SANS INDIVIDUALS/ A MASS OF HUMANS

JS/O7/ M378/This marble monument is erected by the State

What is given above is a person's identity inscribed by the government of the State as the epitaph on the tomb. The person is the main character in W. H. Auden's famous poem, 'The Unknown Citizen'. He was found to be the best citizen of the State. The official explanation about him when he was in service ran like this: 'According to the report from Bureau of Statistics, there was not even a single complaint registered in his name. Later in years, he took up a job in a factory. He had duly made all the payments including the Union fee. His insurance is flawless. His health card says that he was once admitted to the hospital but returned home recovered. As per media reports, he used to follow dutifully everything in the newspapers including advertisements. He had paid his installments in time. He had things like gramophone and refrigerator. He was called 'Saint'. He had five children as decreed by the government.'

The man was a man of no identity or name of his own. A robot like man. The Unknown Citizen. This is what the State wants: Do not think; just obey the State.

The poem ends in this way:

"Was he free?
Was he happy?
The question is absurd.
Had anything been wrong
We should certainly have heard."

The poem, 'The Unknown Citizen' presents the State's project of developing a mass of humans, erasing their individuality. Suppressing the growth of people's individual capacity, the State indoctrinates and subjugates them into obeying its orders like slaves. In countries where there is only a single-party-system, this process is carried out in the most horrendous ways. Of course, in liberal democratic countries people do have the right to choose their political parties but the administration is in bureaucrats' hands. Most of the 'unknown citizens' will have as their only goal ingratiating themselves with the government and, thus, earning its trust. What is good for a nation's progress --- building a uniform society or developing a creative society of diverse talents? Even our fields of Art, Culture and Literature have turned into areas of imitation. The most substantial riches these days are creativity and innovative ideas. The age of Information Technology demands them. Hence, our education must aim at creating the environment for developing our children's creativity and independent thinking. It is exigent that the boring Banking Education should be controlled and that students should be given increasing opportunities to compete with themselves. The system of education that sends out at the cost of billions an army of jobseekers with a degree certificate and without any vocational training must be checked. Also, the system of government recruitment of employees based on irrelevant General Knowledge Tests and on nominal interviews must be stopped. Using their power and influence, the bureaucrats in government departments are preventing the real experts from serving the society.

From Health to Education wherever they find an opportunity to make monetary gains, the avaricious lobbies will flourish. The first thing they do in this case is to make that area available only for people with 'certificates'. For instance, the construction field. Even if one is an excellent architect, unless one is not a draftsman with an approved certificate, one's plan will not be accepted. A few years back, almost all villages did not need license or permit for constructing a building. But today they need it. Just compare the constructions before permit was not needed and after it was needed. Those beautiful buildings including palaces and homesteads standing in harmony with Nature and constructed by ancient architects centuries ago remain intact even today. But these architects would not be able to submit a plan legally even in a *Panchayat* , even if they followed all the laws concerning building construction because they had no 'certificate'. As per the government, 'the draftsman certificate' is considered greater than the innate talent and skills acquired through decades of training.

This bureaucratic stand is spreading into other fields even in other countries. In many countries a law is being enacted that 'certificates' are needed for running a barbershop or a beauty parlor. If the law is implemented, the traditional barbers, carpenters and cooks will become 'fakes'. It will be no surprise if one has to have a degree in Music for singing and if one without the degree is called a 'fake' singer. When I see orchestras and 'reality shows' spinning money, I feel that a time will come when it is insisted that only singers with degree in Music should sing professionally. In such a scenario, our naturally gifted singer will have to be content with singing at home.

Once we examine every field of profession, we can see how brain drain happens in our society. In old days, geniuses were recruited into kings' courts on the basis of their virtuosity. To facilitate the recruitment, week-long debates of scholars and gatherings of virtuosos were conducted. This was the reason why the brilliant kings and their courts of the olden days were of higher standards. *Vedavyasa, Valmiki, Charaka, Shushrutha, Aryabhatta, Bhaskara, Thyagaraja an Swathithirunaal* bear witness to the fact that our ancient systems of society and education had enough opportunities in them for brilliant people to grow. Why does today's society which we call 'modern' fail to produce such geniuses? The answer to this relevant question is simple: Today, powers that be are in their position not because of excellence but because of passing exams by rote-learning questions and answers. The people who implemented the system of 'certificate' were well aware of its drawbacks. That is why they didn't implement it in higher echelons of governance and legislative assemblies.

Modern science has worked wonders in the world, but it has to do more in harmony with Nature and its creatures. Modern science is not yet convinced of its limitations in interfering with Nature and its phenomena. It should realize that it shouldn't be hostile to nature and that we are just one species among millions of species that have equal rights. Each scientific activity must ensure that it does not harm in any way Nature or the coming generations. What we needs science with a sense of ethics. Another thing to be considered is our approach to knowledge. Along with realizing that every creature, including the ant, has intelligence, we should acknowledge the insights and practical intelligence of all humans with gumption. We should not have the narrow view that only those who have passed examinations by rote-learning the questions and answers prepared by the system of government have knowledge.

We need to build 'smart villages' that have pure air, clean water, honest people, birds, animals, agriculture and Wi-Fi , not 'smart cities' costing trillions that are uninhabitable because of pollution and wastage. Let us, who enlightened the world from time immemorial, present to the world a new development model in harmony with Nature.

BE FANS OF AFFLUENCE

All most all our movements have as their slogan, 'eradication of poverty' and as their main theme, 'poverty'. For decades, they have been talking about the poor and poverty. In a system of democracy, political parties need popular support. It would seem that political parties are competing with each other to assure that they are with the poor.

When such a political party held a meeting to explain things, a follower asked his leader, "Isn't our party one that strives for a world of wealth and the wealthy?" The leader, then, became furious with the follower. He said, "I think you have become a fan of the high class and the bourgeoisie." Immediately, the follower corrected himself and said apologetically, "Oh, no, we are striving for a world of poverty and the poor." It was then that the leader understood his blunder.

Many of our political parties manage to survive in the name of the poor. But our goal should not be to create more and more poor people. We need more and more rich people. Our aim must be to make every citizen rich, not only materially but also mentally and intellectually. Our goal must be a world of riches and the rich. What we worship must be what is good. We worship good songs and singers. We worship good acting and actors. In the same way, let us worship 'good' affluence and affluent people. By 'good' I mean 'ethical'.

Unfortunately, most of our political parties worship material wealth. But even the frontline leaders of many political parties, though they themselves are rich, dare not 'openly' adore or appreciate the rich who are 'good'. The wealthy and wealth of a nation has a significant place in that nation's progress.

So, we should not keep the poor all their life poor by giving certain concessions; we should make the poor rich. Let us worship affluence; let us strive for a world of affluence and the affluent.

PRACTICE JOY

All over the world these days we see a number of training programs and trainers in connection with many areas in daily life. Their services help many people. The secrets of happiness and the way to be happy are some of the important concerns in these programs. Everyone aspires to live a happy life. These training programs prove that we have no idea of what joy is and how we can be joyful.

As mentioned in the beginning of this book, we never look into ourselves. Without realizing that joy is within ourselves, we wander outside in search of joy and happiness. We have no idea of joy, happiness or comfort. One of the reasons why we are joyless is that we always live in future. When we pass time thinking of future, we don't realize that we are missing the present and joys of life. All the creatures in the world except humans live in the joy of the present, without the burden of worries and hopes about future. Hence, they live in contentment and happiness.

Another reason for our discontent is the competition in our society. When vie with another, hostility emerges in our mind without our knowledge. It generates agitation in us and destroys our joy.

There is a story in Urdu. There was a rascal in a village, a sadist. He lived all his life, deriving pleasure from harassing others. Eventually, when he was bed-ridden, he gathered the villagers at his home. After apologizing to them, he made a request: "Please take me with the cot, place me in some public place and beat me to pulp. I don't want this village to have another evil man like me." As per his request, the villagers took him to a public place and started to beat him. Right then, a group of policemen arrived and beat the villagers brutally. The man was very happy to see the police beat the villagers. In fact, he had already informed the police that he would be he refused to part with the spade, they insisted on taking it. Then he became indignant and asked them,

"Do you know why I do this?"

"To keep the road and its surroundings clean," said the students

"No. I enjoy working with a spade. If you do the job, how can I enjoy it? When you play football, will you like it if I play in your place?"

His explanation made the students quiet.

There is a great message in this small incident. Whatever job we do, we must enjoy doing it. That is when it becomes effective and joyful. We must be able to transform work into worship.

It is when we are in harmony with Nature that we experience natural and timeless happiness. That is why we go traveling as an escape from worries and boredom. A busy urban life robs people in the city of peace and calm. In such situations, they seek peace in the lap of Nature.

The relaxation we derive from beaches, rivers, backwaters, mountains, cascades, woods, meadows and green fields is rejuvenating. It is when they are in the lap of Nature that our poets, artists and painters find it easy to express themselves creatively. Even if may have done creative works in multi-storied buildings in bustling cities, the real core of their inspiration is always Nature.

Urban life is full of external attractions. The totally mechanical life in the cities is in fact dreary. The pure life immersed in nature is the most joyful.

Modern facilities and systems of communications are today available all over the world, irrespective of villages and cities. Our country is full of beautiful, rich villages. We should focus on developing a happy rural life in which rural indigenousness and bucolic beauty are sustained and modern facilities deployed. Our journey from now onwards must be from the cities of unclean air and water to the 'smart villages' of clean air and water. There we will be as safe and happy as we are in mother's lap. Since it is there where the totality of the five elements that form the basis of life lies, let us now chant as a mantra, '*Graamam Gacchaami*' ---- let us go to the village --- let us return to the bucolic.

BIBLIOGRAPHY

1. English Literature, Albert C. Baugh & Thomas Cable
2. Education in England - a Brief History, Derek Gillard
3. A History of English Education in India, Syed Mahmood
4. *Ashtopanishatthukal*, T. Sivashankaran Nair, Mathrubhoomi Books
5. Pedagogy of the Oppressed, Paulo Freier
6. *Vidyabhyasam Bharathatthil* , K. T. Mohammed, Kerala Bhasha Institute
7. *Thuranna Klassmuri*, K. T. Margaret, Kerala Shasthra Sahithya Parishad
8. *Keralatthinte Vikasanam – a few thoughts* -, Ed: K. R. Janardanan, Kerala Shasthra Sahithya parishad.
9. Indian Scientific Heritage, Dr. N. Gopalakrishnan
10. Macbeth, William Shakespeare
11. Unknown Citizen, W. H. Auden
12. *Geetha Darshan – Sankhya Yoga*, Osho

AFTERWORD

This book, *'Graamam Gacchami'* (Back to the Bucolic) is a sequel to 'Swadeshi.edu' published in English in 2018. Besides comparing the Indian Education System and the Western Education System, the book discusses some of my scattered thoughts about the fruitlessness of modern science and civilization based on Western Philosophical System. I do hope that my readers will positively receive this humble effort of mine.

I am ineffably indebted and thankful to the Madaadhipathi of Kolathur Adwaithaashramam, Shrimad Chidananda Puri Swami who blessed me by reading this book meticulously in the midst of his busy schedule and writing an invaluable and meaningful note.

I am equally indebted and grateful to the Ex-minister of Education and member of C.P.I (M). Politbureau, Mr. M.A. Baby who wrote another educative preface to the book. Also, I express my gratitude beyond words to Dr. C.V. Shreekumar who has made a holistic review of the book.

Besides, I also thank from the bottom of my heart Mr. Gopinath for helping me in the discussion on the structure of the book, Mr. Madhu Kizhakkayil for reading the proof, Mr. Sainul Abid & Mr. Najmuddeen (De-sign, Eranakulam) for the lovely design and layout of the book and the owner of Insight Publica, Mr. Sumesh for printing the book beautifully.

Girish Chandran

beaten and that he had to be protected without delay. Even in his state of weakness, he was just thinking of harassing others to make himself happy.

'Sadism', finding pleasure in others' misery, is found only in humans. People cannot find joy in the growth and progress of others. In fact, the growth and progress of others snuff out their joy.

Another factor that drives away happiness from our life is the competitive practices on which our existing social and educational systems are based. One who finds no satisfaction in things one has and chases achievements will have no space for happiness in one's mind.

Once a rich man approached a master and said, "I've earned a lot of money but I am not content." After listening to him, the master called a small child and gave him a fruit. The child kept it in its hand. Then the master gave him another fruit. The child kept it in its next hand. When the master gave him a third fruit, the child found it difficult to take it. He tried to take it after clasping the other two fruits close to its chest. Soon all the fruits fell down to the ground. The master, showing this to the rich man, said, "Take with joy only that you need. Leave anything that is needless. Else, you will lose even what you have." We will have joy and satisfaction only if we train our mind to be satisfied with what we have got.

We should realize that there is joy not only in indulgence but also in abstinence. The factor that drives us to live is joy. When we have no joy, we may even think of ending our life. The only creatures that put an end to their own lives are only the humans. And, the reason is boredom or discontent. Most people live today in the hopes of future, without living in the present. When our hopes about future turn fruitless, we lose our self-assurance and think of killing ourselves.

We ourselves have to decide our joy. Our life often looks boring when the jobs we do are boring. Late Mr. C. Krishnan Nair of my village, *Poyilkkaav,* was a U.P. School teacher and trustee of the village temple. He was known as 'Swami Krishnan Master', as he used to live like a monk. A bachelor, he lived in the temple. On his return from school, he would go to temple-compound with a spade. He would either do some tilling or clean the road and the temple premises. Once when he was cleaning the road, some of his old students came by car. They tried to take the spade from him to help him out. When